## Letting go of your marriage...and letting God.

In *Cementing the Torn Strands,* Jeenie Gordon frankly addresses the negative feelings that can prevent recovery from divorce and presents an alternative: positive steps toward healing.

She candidly shares from her own experience that you have the choice — to "end up either bitter or better" by:

- Giving up the right to revenge
- Learning to wait
- Overcoming guilt
- Embracing faith, hope, and humor

*Cementing the Torn Strands* shows you how to relinquish your marriage into God's loving hands so He can give you something better.

# CEMENTING
## the
# TORN
# STRANDS

## JEENIE GORDON

Fleming H. Revell Company
Tarrytown, New York

Scripture identified KJV is from the King James Version of the Bible.

Scripture identified NAS is from the New American Standard Bible, © The Lockman Foundation 1960, 1962, 1963, 1968, 1971, 1972, 1973, 1975, 1977.

Scripture identified RSV is from the Revised Standard Version of the Bible, Copyrighted © 1946, 1952, 1971, by the Division of Christian Education of the National Council of the Churches of Christ in the United States of America, and is used by permission. All rights reserved.

All names of persons whose stories are shared have been changed, as have their situations, in order to protect their privacy.

Library of Congress Cataloging-in-Publication Data
Gordon, Jeenie.
    Cementing the torn strands / Jeenie Gordon.
        p.   cm.
    ISBN 0-8007-5409-3
    1. Divorced people—Religious life.   2. Divorce—Religious aspects—Christianity.   3. Gordon, Jeenie.   I. Title.
BV4596.D58G67   1991
248.8'46—dc20                                             91-12402
                                                              CIP

Copyright © 1991 by Jeenie Gordon
Published by the Fleming H. Revell Company
Tarrytown, New York 10591
Printed in the United States of America

TO Kathi Lundstrom,
my precious daughter and dearest friend.
Thank you for your love and encouragement.

# ACKNOWLEDGMENTS

Thank you to

My extended family and friends for their interest, support, and love.

Noted Christian writer and Gold Medallion recipient Norman Rohrer, my mentor.

Authors Lee Roddy, who believed I could write, and Sherwood Wirt, who suggested the book.

# CONTENTS

# PREFACE

This is a book about hope!

Running for the telephone, I picked it up to hear the cheery voice of a former client. "Jeenie, " she bubbled, "you'd never believe how good my life is now. I remember what you taught me in therapy, and I use it all the time. In fact, I'm passing it on to my friends. They're changing, too."

This is my desire for you: an emotionally healthy life-style. As you put these concepts into practice, God will bring beauty out of the ashes of your life.

Several years after my divorce, I was involved in an automobile accident (August 16, 1980) that could have taken my life. On August 16, *1990* (ten years to the day), my contract was drawn for this book. It was as if God said, "Look what I've done with your life in ten years."

He will come through for you, too!

# FOREWORD

Picture venerable old Solomon browsing in a modern book-store. He peels book after book off the shelves and views the same themes that troubled him so long ago: Keeping Marriage Joys Alive, Getting the Most Out of Life, How to Really Love Your Mate, Why Do Couples Fight? When Love Dies. . . .

The Preacher sighs and reaches for yet another book. This one intrigues. It offers hope not merely from someone who has pulled together a lot of platitudes but from someone who has known deep suffering herself and has found the answers to recovery. With a smile, Solomon takes the book to the counter, lays down a gold coin, and wanders out to find a quiet place to read.

Like Solomon, Jeenie Gordon experienced life on the ragged edge. Once launched into a happy marriage, she saw her dreams crumble when the man she trusted to keep his wedding vows left her. Instead of becoming bitter, the author of this book decided to prepare herself to make a difference in the lives of others by helping them to rebuild their shattered lives.

After earning two degrees in the field of counseling and administration, Jeenie plunged into her ministry of agape love. As a certified counselor she went into prisons, hospitals, convalescent homes, offices, and schools.

In private practice and in the employ of high school administrations, she has spent many hours listening and analyzing, explaining and prescribing, praying and pointing the way to the Giver of life and hope eternal. Jeenie has helped hundreds of people learn to love again—not to get what they want but to become what they ought to be.

I am proud to have been an encourager along the way when Jeenie took her first halting steps into the world of writing. She stayed with the project until every fact was checked, every reference corroborated, and every principle tested in the Refiner's fire.

Like Solomon, Jeenie "went on teaching the people all she knew . . . in an interesting manner." Get ready to enjoy her practical wisdom as you read how to acquire emotional health and how to make the most of the remainder of your life, no matter what has gone before.

NORMAN B. ROHRER

# 1

# HOW CAN I SURVIVE?

Quietly shuffling into the lobby amid the somber strains of organ music, I felt enormous anger. The tears seeping from the corners of my half-closed eyes mixed with the fury burning inside my stomach and the never-ending ache in my heart.

As I gingerly peered into the face of the deceased, I saw him not as a corpse but as an alive, vibrant man. His love for his wife was honest. He was faithful, vigorous, humorous, and tender. They touched, they laughed, they loved. I envied their marriage—oh, how I envied it.

Now his widow was being treated with great tenderness. Soon she would be receiving casseroles, condolences, and cards of sympathy. Knowing she had been intensely loved by her husband added to my rage and self-pity.

Two years previously, my husband had left. I was rejected, unloved, and received minimal support. There are no covered dishes or Hallmark cards for those in the pain of divorce. It isn't fair!

My emotions were screaming, *Why did he leave? I feel so rejected. Why couldn't I have been truly loved? I was never number one. It's so unjust. I wish he had died instead. At least I'd have loving memories—I could live with that. But not with divorce.*

Rejection is the most painful aspect of a separation and divorce. We feel turned inside out with the raw, bloody edges being scrutinized by an uncaring, busy world. Life has lost its meaning. Nothing matters. No one wants to hear how much it hurts. They pretend it will soon be okay, glibly quote Bible verses, and say, "Time will heal." It doesn't help—nothing does. The deathly stillness of rejection becomes a black, hooded cloak with only a pair of pain-filled eyes visible.

When a spouse dies, the pain is enormous and the separation permanent. There is a definite ending. With closure comes support from a caring community. In divorce, this seldom occurs.

Most divorced couples continue to be in contact, yet rarely in a positive way. Phone calls and letters may be full of blame, hate, disrespect, and harassment. This keeps the feelings stirred and slows down the healing process.

Rejection is an extremely painful, tearing experience. It is difficult to think you are no longer loved by someone who promised "forever." Perhaps you have pleaded and begged for the marriage to continue and tried everything you could—yet, it failed. You feel disrespected, disappointed, hurt, as though your guts have been ripped out. Rejection has slung you against the wall of an out-of-control elevator of emotions, all on the downward plunge. You feel helpless, hopeless, and don't care about anything or anyone. "I just want the hurting to stop!" you scream.

"Where is God?" you thunder. "What have I done to deserve this? I don't understand. I can't stand the pain."

The good news is that there is healing!

## Steps to Healing

Dr. Elisabeth Kübler-Ross's theory of the healing process (*On Death and Dying*, Macmillan, 1969) is applicable to any of life's traumas, including divorce.

*Acceptance*

*Deep Depression*

*Bargaining*

*Anger*

*Denial*

I prefer to put these stages into stair steps rather than a circle, for in this process, we go up and down these steps many times before reaching final acceptance. In just one hour, we can be up and down these stages over and over. Also, the steps are not always experienced in this exact order.

In therapy, I may hear a client say, "I could kill that sucker. She's made my life so miserable. She doesn't deserve to live. As a matter of fact, I don't, either. If I had the guts, I'd blow my brains out. But you know, I still feel in my heart she'll be back someday. She just needs more time. In a few years, it will all work out."

In this illustration, the person began in *anger*, jumped to *depression*, and ended the statement in *denial* in only ten seconds.

As you progress through the stages, you will spend a smaller amount of time in each stage, and there will be longer pain-free periods between.

Healing is curtailed if a stage is skipped. For instance, because

I did not allow myself to feel and express anger for nearly two years, healing did not occur as rapidly as was possible. I was on a detour.

The first step is *Denial*. There is a feeling you will wake up from this bad dream. This disaster is really not true. You keep thinking, *I can't believe this. This can't be happening to me. It only happens to other people. This can't be real.*

Denial is a vital part of the healing process. It is the period of being in shock. The pain is dulled. In an accident, a person in shock may not feel physical pain. It is nature's way of anesthetizing for a time. In the same manner, emotional pain is numbed to some extent during the Denial stage. It is possible to be stuck at that stage.

A man came to me for therapy after his wife left him for another man. Two years later, he still believed his wife would come back to him, even though she blatantly stated over and over that she would not leave her lover. His children encouraged him to get on with his life, but he refused.

One day he was found slumped over his desk after suffering a heart attack. During his hospital stay, his wife was by his side constantly (probably out of guilt). She was kind and loving, even to the point of moving back home for a few days. While my client was recuperating, she left, stating that she was going back to her boyfriend for good.

A short time ago, my client's wife admitted to him numerous affairs she had had during their marriage. Still this gentleman hangs on to his belief that she will come back. He is unwilling to step out of denial. How sad!

Another stage is *Anger*. This anger is horrendous, explosive, and expressive. It is rage against being violated by one you love and fury that your spouse would reject you when you have tried so hard and wanted the marriage so desperately.

The opposite of love is not hate. Apathy is the opposite of love. Hate and anger are felt because the love is so deep and the hurt so intense.

I did not encounter this stage (to a healthy degree) until two years after my marriage ended. My anger threshold was very high because I continued to deny feelings. I did not know I was a very angry person.

It was an ordinary day when my anger began to surface. Throughout the day, my thoughts continued. By late afternoon, I was enraged at my former husband.

*I'd like to go over to his office and give him a piece of my mind*, I thought. My next idea was, *I'll wait until tomorrow* (my usual passive response). *No*, I argued, *if you don't go now, you won't be mad enough to say what needs to be said.* So, I went.

My heart was palpitating, my palms were sweaty, and I felt as if cotton were stuffed in my mouth. I rounded the corner to his office, hoping his car would not be there. I was relieved beyond words—no car. Then, to my horror, I noticed he had parked in a different place.

Entering the building, I walked into his office unannounced. Shock and disbelief were etched across his face. I'm sure his heart was doing some pounding to match the throbbing of my own.

"I need to talk with you," I began. The look on my face was not to be taken lightly. He offered me a seat.

Resolutely, I began to express my anger because of his rejection and choice to leave the marriage. Nothing was held back. My enormous rage came from deep within me. I was incapable of squelching my fury.

This was a positive step in healing.

I grew up suppressing anger. It was important to me to please, to be good, not to make waves. Because of a rather legalistic church upbringing, I thought the expression of anger was sinful. So, as time went on, irritations were consistently "swept under the rug."

Numerous people come into my counseling office who have spent their lives repressing anger. It causes havoc in one's life and relationships.

When we are unwilling to state our angry feelings and thoughts, there is a buildup of resentment and bitterness.

After anger is verbalized, it needs to be resolved. Joan was a classic example of unresolved anger. Her husband left her with five small children and moved in with his lover. She seethed, screamed, screeched, and spit four-letter words at him. Resolution, not repression, was her problem.

Joan's divorce settlement gave her the family home plus an income that would meet all their needs until the children were grown. Her budget included a weekly housekeeper and gardener.

Since Joan had married prior to completing her college degree, her desire was to finish school. I encouraged her to attain this goal. She began taking a full college class load.

Seldom have I encountered a woman who was angrier or more bitter. Time and time again, through clenched teeth she spewed forth the words, "I hate him. I will *never* forgive him. Never! Not as long as I live. Never!"

She didn't. Ten years later, Joan contacted me and expressed many of the same angry statements I had heard earlier. She had not completed her degree because she chose to continually drop courses. She had gone from job to job and stated she was usually fired because of her attitude. Her children were grown. The spousal and child support were depleted. She was bitter, alone, and desperate.

The third step is *Bargaining*. This may come in a variety of forms. You say such things as, "If only I had . . ." or "Why didn't I . . ." or "If only I had said . . ." and so on, trying to convince yourself if you had done things differently, the divorce would not have occurred. You would still be loved and accepted.

Sue's husband of thirty-five years left her for another woman. In a moment of honesty, her spouse disclosed she had been a wonderful wife and mother. Sue, however, wants to believe she could have done more. She constantly tells me, "I usually had a clean home and a good dinner ready for him. Sometimes, though, the house was a bit messy, and once in a while I didn't spend a lot of time on the meal. If it had been perfect for him, he wouldn't have left me. I really failed him. I didn't do enough. He told me I wasn't as much fun sexually as the other woman. I thought we had a really good sex life. I was responsive and tried to please him, but I'm just no good."

Sue continues to dissect and scrutinize every inch of her life trying to find the "reason" he left. She will never find an answer. The fact is that Sue was a good wife and mother, as her husband admitted. He, however, chose to end the marriage.

We also bargain with God. We desperately pray, "God, if you put this marriage back together, I promise You I will. . . ." God does not bargain with us. Nor will He override a mate's choice to leave the marriage. God gives each of us the right to make our own decisions, even if they are wrong and will inflict pain. He has created us to be free moral agents, which gives us the freedom to choose.

The naked truth is that bargaining doesn't work and *Deep Depression* sets in. This is another stage of healing. During this time, the pain is overwhelming, excruciating, unbearable. Sui-

cide is often a thought and, to some, an act. During this de-
pressive stage, most people do not want to live. They may not
contemplate suicide actively, but the will to go on has van-
ished.

In working with hundreds of separated and divorced people, I
cannot count the times I have received desperate suicidal calls.
One call in particular is etched in my memory. I was gone for the
evening and the message was left on my recorder. "Jeenie, are
you there? Answer me. Are you there? I can't live anymore. I
need you. Please, please answer me. I want to die." The person
made three attempts to reach me with the same agonizing message.

I arrived home in the early morning. As I listened to the telephone recording, my heart was pounding and I cried, "Please,
God, let this precious person still be alive." My hand was shaking as I took the receiver and dialed. What a relief to hear my call
answered. We talked at length and got through another night.

Feeling depressed is normal at this stage. If these feelings were
not occurring, it would be a sign of deep psychological problems.
You are not going crazy! It is important to feel the pain. Walk
through it—don't run. Allow healing to begin. Feel what you
feel: anguish, abandonment, agony. Get in touch with feelings
rather than denying them. Let tears flow. They help to flush the
pain and are beneficial to healing.

The final stage is *Acceptance.* You may be looking at this
statement and thinking, *No way. I'm not capable of this, and
quite truthfully, I don't* want *to accept it.*

It is all right to feel that way. If you are recently separated or
divorced, it is not imperative to confront this issue right away. Be
kind to yourself. It takes time—lots of time. Allow yourself all
the time you need to heal.

One day, however, even though the loss is great and some of the pain still momentarily occurs, you will have an underlying sense it will be okay. You will begin to tell yourself, *I can survive. I can heal.*

Healing is a choice.

# Insight for Growth

1. You are sitting in a room alone with your spouse. Your feelings are banging around in your stomach like a cement mixer.
   Tell your mate how you *really* feel. Don't hold anything
   back—scream it out.

2. What things make you furious about the separation or divorce?

3. Describe what scares you.

4. Express the feelings you are having *right now*. Put names to them: "I feel . . ." (furious, disappointed, pain, worried, abandoned, unloved, undesirable, disrespected, fear).

# 2

# LETTING GO OF THE MARRIAGE

As I drove cautiously into my garage, my sixteen-year-old dog waddled toward me with the hint of a tail wag. Lady was my buddy, my constant companion, whom I adored. The last few days she had not felt well, but usually she would bounce back quickly. As I peered more closely into her soft brown eyes, I realized she was very ill. Snuggling her in my arms, I sensed she was almost comatose. My heart jumped as I said, "My dog is dying."

Gently, tenderly, I laid her in my car. Tears came in torrents as I stroked her limp body on the seat next to me. As I drove, I made the painful decision that, if she were seriously ill, I would have her put to sleep.

The veterinarian found that Lady's kidneys had failed; he could hospitalize her and operate, but there wasn't much hope. Perhaps she could live a few more days. He asked what I wanted to do.

"I've made my decision," I said. "I want you to put her to

sleep while I am here with her.'' The tears were cascading from my eyes, plummeting down my face. I could hardly see. Both the vet and his assistant were handing me tissues.

The doctor prepared the serum. I patted my dog lovingly while he injected. In a few moments, her breathing stopped. He said, ''She's gone. I'll leave you alone with her for a bit.''

As the tears were splashing on her lifeless form, I tenderly slid my fingers through Lady's gray fur and took off her collar and name tag. ''God,'' I cried, ''thank You for the years I've had my Lady. She has been such a precious little pal to me—a special gift from You.''

For two days I cried enormous tears. It was almost as though I were ''throwing up'' the pain inside as it came spurting out.

Previously, in life's traumas, I had always been one who ''held up well.'' I let my pain *seep* out rather than gush. In fact, I was rather disgusted with people who became hysterical in their pain.

When Lady died, however, I learned a valuable lesson. By my willingness to be overwrought and let the pain come out in a swirling force, I began to feel better. Conversely, after my separation and divorce, I only allowed my pain to seep out in droplets and, in doing so, hindered and lengthened the healing process.

The first step in letting go of a marriage is to intensely *feel* the pain, to experience it fully, be encompassed by it, let it run its course. Only when you experience the density of pain can it be released explosively.

In my opinion, cultures who express pain with loud crying, beating of chests, and wailing have a healthy outlet. They are able to heal more quickly because they really ''get into'' their pain.

# Choosing to Let Go

Letting go is difficult. I truly wish there were a surefire formula, but there is none. However, I want to help you understand the process and to give you encouragement to get on with life. During the working-through period (denial, anger, bargaining, depression, acceptance), letting go is occurring.

Dejectedly, a client professed, "I'm so unhappy. I really wish I had stuck out the marriage rather than divorcing." She had been divorced six years. For years, her husband had blatantly flaunted his numerous affairs to her, their family, and friends. He was currently living with a teenage girlfriend.

It was sad to think that, after this woman had endured disrespect for years, she would rather have continued in a relationship of victimization rather than be divorced. It said something very significant to me. She had not let go of the marriage and preferred contempt rather than building a new life for herself.

Growth is a choice; healing is a decision—so is letting go. We cannot control what happened, but we choose our response to the event.

In choosing to let go, we also have a decision to make regarding how we will grieve. There is a difference between positive mourning and negative mourning.

Negative grief entails a lot of self-pity. At times, self-pity does creep into our thoughts, but the damage occurs when we continue to dwell on it. Someone has said, "Self-pity is the lowest form of human entertainment."

Positive grief is composed of doing things that will get our lives back together. We've heard the adage, "Time heals." I think that's a stupid statement. Time does not heal. It passes. What we *choose* to do while time passes is the important factor. We need to do things that bring about the healing process.

Jim Smoke, author of *Growing Through Divorce*, believes it takes a minimum of two years to recover from a divorce. In counseling hundreds of divorced singles, I concur. Therefore, there is a lot we can do in two years that will help ensure coming through a divorce as a healthy and whole person.

## Should I Hope?

How does hope fit, or does it? You may be asking, "Are you telling me I have to accept this divorce, even when I don't want it, and that there is no hope?" No, I am not.

However, the only hope for a marriage in trouble, in my opinion, is when each partner is willing to work on the problems in counseling, so the marriage can become one that is healthy, rewarding, and good.

It takes two people who want a marriage. Often one partner is asking for the divorce and is unwilling to work at restoration. Unless both husband and wife are desirous of therapy and commit to being open, honest, and vulnerable during the sessions, the marriage has little chance for survival.

Six days prior to our anniversary, I learned of my husband's discontent. With a crushed but hopeful heart, I penned the following prose and gave it to him on our anniversary:

> Their lives were shattered, hope was gone, darkness flooded their dreams. Two hearts once united were torn to shreds—tears became a torrent of winter rain. The break was too wide, scarring until it was unrecognizable—too deep to ever be sutured for a continued or new life together.
>
> But the Master came. Gently wiping the tearstained eyes, He began to carefully mend—slowly but deliberately. He encountered difficulty in cementing the ragged, torn strands.

As they lay quietly and trustingly in His hands, the restored hearts began to take on a surprisingly new form—He
made them into one!

After several unsuccessful visits with two marriage counselors,
I was still adamant about saving the marriage. It seemed impossible for me to admit there was no hope. The thought was too
painful.

My hopes were high, yet the marriage ended.

In my private practice as a therapist, there have been times I
worked with only one spouse yet saw the marriage turn around.
I believe we all live in systems. When one person in a system
begins to change, all the others in his system can no longer relate
in the old ways. They, too, begin to change.

In a counseling session with a woman named Sally, I observed
the tenseness of her body and the facial fury as she spit out, "I'm
only here to get up the courage to leave my husband. The marriage is rotten and I want out."

During the next year, I saw phenomenal growth. Sally was
willing to deal with her own issues. She learned how to communicate her needs and thoughts to her spouse in a nonthreatening
way. Instead of shouting, "You make me so mad, you jerk!" she
used an "I message": "Honey, I need to talk to you about
yesterday. I felt put down when you cursed me out because I
asked you to take out the trash. I probably was nagging and I
don't want to act that way, but I was really angry at your response. I felt disrespected and unloved by you."

She developed additional good communication skills and put
them into practice. Even though her spouse came only once for
therapy, the marriage began to grow. Honesty prevailed, bonding
occurred, fun emerged, trust grew, sex became exciting.

Because Sally changed, so did her system (husband and children). With a smile sprinting across her face, she expressed, "I am so glad I didn't get a divorce. I never would have dreamed a marriage could be this good."

Even though it is possible for a marriage to heal through the individual therapy of one spouse, it is usually more effective for the couple to have conjoint counseling in order to work on specific areas in the relationship together.

Finally, if there is a third party involved in the marital breakup, the chances of restoration are slim. Generally, the need for security is too strong to abandon the marriage unless there is someone waiting in the wings. It gives the partner the courage to leave, and the possibility of the marriage being restored is extremely slight.

A further word: For some, there is no lover waiting. They choose to leave the marriage because of continual emotional/physical abuse, alcoholism, drug addiction, or infidelity. It takes enormous courage to remove oneself (temporarily or permanently) from an emotionally damaging situation.

## The Stuff I Tell Myself

Dr. Albert Ellis, a noted psychotherapist, developed a theory and labeled it the ABCs. Christian psychologist Dr. David Stoop, in his book *Self Talk: Key to Personal Growth*, talks about the principle of Self-Talk.

Simply stated:

A is the *Activating Event*. This is the event that has brought discomfort, pain, or trauma. It is causing a problem.

C are the *Consequences*. Our culture tends to think the Activating Event *causes* us to act or feel in predictable ways—that Consequences are a direct result of the Activating Event. In other words, A = C.

This thinking brings about unhealthy attitudes and actions. For example, if a divorce were the Activating Event:

| A | C |
|---|---|
| *Activating Event* | *Consequences* |
| Divorce | A life without love |
|  | No spouse or prospects |
|  | Desperation |
|  | Eternal loneliness |
|  | Life is over |

However, the key to the ABC Theory is B (the *Belief System*). The consequences are produced by what we *think* about the Activating Event. So,

| A | B | C |
|---|---|---|
| *Activating Event* | *Belief System* | *Consequences* |
| Divorce | Life is over | Hopelessness |

We cannot change the Activating Event, but we can change our Belief System about the event, thus changing the Consequences. For instance:

| A | B | C |
|---|---|---|
| *Activating Event* | *Belief System* | *Consequences* |
| Divorce | "This is not disaster; I will survive" | A new, fulfilled life |

It is not uncommon to place blame elsewhere, for it lets us off the hook. If we view ourselves as victims of circumstance, we can abdicate our responsibility to change and grow. While I was teaching a Divorce Recovery seminar at a Christian conference center, a lady raised her hand and said, "I've been separated fourteen years, and I just wonder when I'll be over it." This spurred my curiosity, so I talked with her privately. "How long have you been divorced?" I questioned.

"Actually," she said, "the divorce is not final." The puzzled look on my face prompted her apologetic response: "I've, well, I've never signed the final papers,"she sighed. "But," she continued, "I'm curious to know how long it would take me to heal." My response was, "As long as you choose."

## More on Self-Talk

We converse at approximately two hundred-plus words per minute. We talk to ourselves, however, to the tune of thirteen hundred words per minute. So, even when we're listening, we're talking to ourselves at this high rate of speed.

Proverbs 23:7 reads, "As [a man] thinketh in his heart, so is he" (KJV). Psychologists predict we will become what we are thinking in five years. Some days that sounds wonderful; other days—God forbid.

Our thoughts are derived from what we tell ourselves. This constitutes our belief system. And, like it or not, we have enormous power over our thoughts.

We do not always have control over events, but we have a choice as to our response. Our Belief System, then, brings about the Consequences, good or bad.

If we speak negatively to ourselves about who we are and what we will become, we will eventually begin to believe it. Someday it may actually occur.

Or, we have the choice to encourage ourselves, to entertain

positive thoughts, to believe we can succeed. Soon our lives will begin to change for the better.

Bob came to me for help. He was despondent. His wife had dumped him. He was down on himself, telling himself the most horrible things. He was getting worse, and I was getting desperate. I decided to use a counseling technique called "Rubber Band Psychology."

"Bob," I suggested, "I want you to wear a big, fat rubber band on your wrist. When your negative self-talk begins, snap that sucker—hard." I was relieved when Bob came back the next week to report the therapy was working. He began to break the cycle of destructive self-talk.

Often, I catch myself on a treadmill of negativism and I say aloud, "Stop it, Jeenie." (This concept works best when I'm alone—I've gotten some funny looks when I wasn't.) Sometimes I must do this over and over before I begin to break the pattern.

## New Normal

Even though your marriage may have left a lot to be desired, there was a feeling of normalcy. It felt right, comfortable, okay— like being in a groove.

When separation/divorce occurs, however, we enter a phase of feeling "not normal." This is the time we work through the pain process (denial, anger, bargaining, depression, acceptance). During this period, little feels good or right anymore.

After the Abnormal Phase (working-through process) is accomplished, a new normal is established. Things have changed. They are different yet good. Once again we are happy and content and life has meaning.

After the New Normal is well established, if we were suddenly transported back into the Old Normal, it would feel uncomfortable, for our new life has begun.

When I was married, I liked being in the furrow. It was easy. I knew what to expect, how to act, how to respond.

Entering separation was gut-wrenching. Nearly everything had changed. My feelings were going crazy and, at times, I feared perhaps I was, too. Life was uncertain and scary.

Eventually, I established a new life. I now feel secure, happy, and confident in God and in myself. My life-style is radically different, yet I finally feel okay again.

On occasion, I remember my marriage and can hardly believe that person was me. Even thinking of it evokes a strange emotion. I am healed.

# Humor

Since divorce is such a tumultuous time, humor may be put to rest. During tough times, though, is when it is most needed. We can be truly refreshed when we allow ourselves to enjoy a hearty laugh.

Anne's husband had been flagrant about his infidelities during their marriage. One evening he left to spend time with his girlfriend, she assumed. Anne was enraged. She had had enough of his behavior, so she followed him.

Grabbing her purse and slinging it over one shoulder, she bounded toward her car with hair flying as crazily as she was acting. Revving up the engine, she slapped it into gear and careened down the streets like a wild woman. She knew where this witch lived and broke all speed records getting there.

Ramming the car up to the curb, turning whitewalls into black ones, and slamming on the brakes, she came to a screeching halt.

With pounding heart, sweaty palms, and anger spurting out of every pore, she decided to wait a few minutes.

When her anger could no longer be held, Anne sprang from the car and slammed the door, weakening the hinges and rattling the windows, and bolted up the stairs to the house.

With all the calm she could possibly muster, she rang the bell. When no one answered, her fury was uncontainable. With tightened fists she banged on the door, pounding and screaming for them to open up. Of course, they didn't respond.

She was now in a frame of mind to stop at nothing. Racing to the back of the house and finding the door locked, she continued to pound and yell. It did no good. She made a quick decision.

On her belly she squeezed, wiggled, and crawled through the doggy door, slid raging into the bedroom, and demanded that her husband come home!

Driving home, Anne laughed hysterically over her antics. So have hundreds of others, as I've related the tale.

A final word: Unless you let go and release your former spouse, God can give you nothing better.

# Insight for Growth

1. You are sitting on a sofa across from me. We are alone. Tell me what your pain feels like.




2. Your spouse enters the room. Tell your mate how you *really* feel. Leave nothing unsaid. Scream, cry, yell if you must, but get it out.

3. We are alone again. Why are you hanging on to the marriage? Give me all your reasons and your feelings.

4. Just between us, what would happen if you let go?

# 3

# DEALING WITH THE FORMER SPOUSE

He shuffled into my office with lowered head and slumped shoulders. As he sank on to the couch, he tilted his head toward the ceiling. Tears fell, cascading down his sculptured, strong face. Deep pain escaped his lips as he whispered, "I really believed she was back—that she wanted me and our marriage.

"The aloneness was more than I could cope with," he continued, "so I called her to see if she wanted to go out for dinner. When she accepted, I was overjoyed. We had this great meal and talked for hours—just like old times. We ended up in bed. It was so good, such great sex."

*Then why,* I thought, *do I see such anguish on his face?* He continued, "This morning she left. Said she doesn't love me and was going back to her lover. I don't understand. Why? How could she do this to me?"

# The Clean Break

Making a clean break goes against every fiber of our being because we want to hold on and to make the marriage work. Our desperation screams, "Hang in there, keep on trying, do whatever the spouse wants."

When a spouse dies, the clean break is done for us. In a divorce, *we* must do it. That's why it is such a gut-wrenching experience.

When a spouse has decided to leave the marriage and pursue divorce, I believe there should be a definite severing by the rejected mate. Many marriages go on with nothing settled. The pain increases, and a divorce is the eventual result.

Making a clean break is deciding you are a worthwhile, deserving person and will no longer allow yourself to be trampled and disrespected by your spouse.

In honesty, state, "I love you intensely and want this marriage. I am willing to work hard in counseling to bring it together into a healthy relationship. I didn't beg you to marry me, nor can I keep you in the marriage against your will. If you choose to divorce, my hurt will be enormous, but I will go on. I will build a new life for myself and one day I will be healed. The door is open. You may go or stay."

The night my husband walked out, the emotional tearing held a stranglehold on my feelings, wrapped rigidly around my body, and permeated my thoughts. Even though my being was enveloped with suffering, there was a sense that God had removed him, for I was incapable of ending the marriage. It seemed as though God had closed the door and, in awe of a holy God, I could not reopen it. Even though I experienced several years of loneliness and pain, I never asked my husband to return.

Often there is a feeling of entrapment by the spouse who chooses to leave the marriage. In contrast, the rejected mate tries desperately to keep the partner from leaving.

To illustrate this point, imagine a friend coming from behind and giving you a quick hug. As he quickly released you, you probably would think, *Oh, how nice,* and you might return the embrace.

Now, instead, envision the friend not letting go. Each time you move or give a nervous laugh, he increases the grip. As he continues to tighten, your dominating thought is, *I have to get away.* Soon you begin to struggle, bend back fingers, wrench yourself from his hold. Because you feel trapped and without a choice, you *have* to get away. There are no other viable options.

In separation, there is a tendency to beg, plead, and hang on to the spouse. When this happens, the partner feels trapped and there is a desperate attempt to go. The permeating thought is to get out of the situation, be free, start over. Not much else matters.

Only when the door is left wide open and the spouse is free to leave will the mate consider any options. The releasing gives opportunity for choice. Some marriages have been turned around because the unhappy partner was given the alternative.

When the mate has the option of leaving, he can stand at the proverbial door and contemplate, "Now that I'm free, is this really what I want? Is it worth giving up all this—the years of love, children, struggling through hard times, joys, memories? Am I crazy to do this? Am I going to live to regret what I've done?"

In scores of marriages, the freedom to choose brought the departing spouse to grips with reality, and the decision was to stay. In counseling couples, I have seen this concept restore the marriage and bring it to a healthy and wholesome state. Dr. James Dobson, in his book *Love Must Be Tough*, expands on this theory in great detail and with expertise.

In tough love, there are two sides to the coin. Love without toughness allows disrespect. Toughness says, "I am worth more than letting you tramp all over my feelings and personhood, and if you do, I will confront you."

Oh, how I wish *Love Must Be Tough* had been written when I needed it! I did all the wrong things—forgave immediately, hardly felt anger (let alone express it), was nonconfrontive, pretended. My responses were unhealthy, but behind them was a right motive and a sincere heart, at least most of the time. Yet my responses were wrong. I've often wondered whether my marriage would have ended in divorce if I had known about and practiced tough-love concepts.

If a separation does occur, a clean break means no sex. Even though there is a great temptation and a person has the right to a sexual relationship while married, it clouds the issues. Couples have gone back and forth for months or years mainly for sexual reasons. The underlying problems are swept under the rug and are not faced realistically and resolved.

One spouse may be sexually involved with another person. If this is the case, the person who wants the marriage will continually be hurt because of the blatant disrespect from the partner. It is important to say, "I respect myself too much to be sexually involved in a threesome."

## Transactional Analysis

Remember the book *I'm O.K.—You're O.K.* by Dr. Thomas A. Harris? It was a raging success in the mid-seventies. The book taught ways to communicate based on whether we were speaking from the position (ego state) of a *Parent*, an *Adult*, or a *Child*.

This theory is called Transactional Analysis, developed by Dr. Eric Berne, and is one model for interpersonal communication.

At best, it is difficult to talk and/or negotiate with a former spouse. Learning some new methods will make the task easier. Not only do these concepts apply to divorced people but they also can be utilized in all interpersonal conversations.

## *The Parent*

The *Parent* part of us contains our values, morals, beliefs, attitudes, and behavior passed on to us from our parents. As an adult, it is important to look at our value system and decide whether it is really our own or merely one adopted from our parents.

The *Parent* has two segments. One side is the *Critical Parent*. It consists of finger pointing, blaming, criticizing, and using words such as *should*, *always*, and *never*. The other half, the *Nurturing Parent*, is caring, encouraging, and cultivates positive growth.

A father came storming into my office with his sixteen-year-old son in tow. He colored the air with four-letter words and debasement of his son because of low grades. When he learned his son had failed a required course two years earlier, it got worse—especially when I questioned why he had not dealt with the grade at the time. Everyone was to blame—me, his son, the school, teachers. I watched the hurt and anger in the teen's eyes. He remained silent.

I asked the young man to remain after his father left. "Tim, it appears you feel helpless around your dad and believe nothing you could say will matter. I see your pain as well as your resentment. It seems your poor grades are a way to get back at your dad.''

Tears began to slide down his face as he nodded affirmation. ''I think you're worth a lot more than that,'' I continued. ''You are a person of value, intelligence, and sensitivity. You're giving yourself a bad deal. I believe in you, Tim, and I want something better for you.'' Then, out of his inner feelings tumbled words expressing a lifetime of built-up, repressed emotions. For an hour he cried and talked.

Tim's father was acting as a *Critical Parent*. My response was a *Nurturing Parent*.

A few weeks later, Tim came breathlessly into my office with his report card. ''I just wanted you to see first. I've raised all my grades—no *D*s,'' he beamed. The next two years, he continued to improve, and I proudly watched him graduate.

Divorce tends to bring out the *Critical Parent* in most of us. It is ugly and damaging. Yet, because of the enormous pain and overwhelming sense of rejection, we scream our blame.

## The Adult

The *Adult* deals with reality, makes logical decisions, organizes, and looks at possibilities.

Communication is difficult enough when things are going well, but when there is a separation/divorce it is horrendous. Emotions run high and play havoc with our logic. It is strenuous and burdensome to try to be rational and step back from our feelings. Most of the time we fail, and all hell breaks loose.

## The Child

There are two parts to the *Child*: the *Natural Child* and the *Adapted Child*.

The *Adapted Child* is either *overcompliant* or *rebellious*. The *Compliant Child* is a people-pleaser and unable to honestly express his needs.

During my marriage, I most frequently responded as a *Compliant Child*, unwilling to make waves, confront, or be honest about thoughts and feelings. I adjusted, then pretended things were wonderful. How dishonest.

Anger is seen most in the *Rebellious Child*. He wants his own way and is manipulative and disrespectful.

A person operating as a *Rebellious Child* has little trouble controlling others or getting his way because people-pleasers are quite anxious to acquiesce.

During the last three years of our marriage, with the knowledge of my husband's unhappiness, I slowly began to grow and change. As my self-esteem expanded, I felt better about myself and was no longer willing to be involved in the game playing.

The *Natural Child* (*Free Child*) is open, honest, uninhibited, willing to express thoughts, desires, and feelings, and is curious and enthusiastic.

When we reach adulthood, we tend to lose touch with the *Natural Child*, which was a vital part of our growing-up years. How sad, because it brings excitement, is challenged by life, explores, plays, is real, honest, vulnerable, joyful, creative, spontaneous, transparent, and enthusiastic. It gives zest to our existence. Childlikeness is God's gift to adults. Conversely, childishness is immature, shirks responsibility, and is hard to get along with.

Watching the teenage box boys at the supermarket jump on the carts and whiz around the parking lot struck a chord in me. One day, coming out of the market with my basket full of groceries, all dressed up from work, I thought, *I don't want to leave this life without having ridden one of those carts.* Another part of me was appalled at the idea and asked, *What if someone sees you?*

I got the basket off to a running start, hopped on, and said, "So what!" The wind whistled through my hair, the sun smiled down on my face, and I was exhilarated as I sped around the lot at .05 miles per hour.

Perhaps riding a shopping basket is not your forte. However, we miss the exhilaration of life when we refuse to let our child-likeness escape in moments of delight. We become boring, less productive, noncreative, and stalemated. Our fear of what people will think can take the fun out of life and the thrill out of new experiences and discoveries.

## How Transactional Analysis Works in Communication

We continually function as *Parent* (*Nurturing* or *Critical*), *Adult*, or *Child* (*Natural* or *Adapted*) in all our relationships.

Here are some examples of a divorcing couple communicating using the *Parent*, *Adult*, and *Child* in an unhealthy mode:

| | |
|---|---|
| *Adult:* | "I'm willing to come to an agreement regarding the house and furniture." |
| *Rebellious Child:* | "You make me sick! All you can think about is money. I hate you." |

This conversation will get nowhere because one of the partners is unwilling to respond as an *Adult*.

If both people spoke from the *Adult* perspective, negotiation of a difficult decision could result:

*Adult:*    "I'm willing to come to an agreement regarding the house and furniture."

*Adult:*    "Me, too. Let's do this in a way that will cause as little damage as possible to each of us and the kids."

Here is an illustration of both persons communicating from a wrong perspective:

*Critical Parent:*    "You should come to see these kids every day! You're a lousy father!"

*Compliant Child:*    "Okay, honey. I will be here every day after work to play with them and tuck them into bed."

In these instances, the *Adapted Child* was either overrebellious or overcompliant. These responses either beat down a former spouse or bring on a fight. Only when the reply is appropriate can communication occur.

A healthy response to the *Critical Parent* might be:

*Critical Parent:*    "You should come to see these kids every day! You're a lousy father!"

*Adult:*    "I am a good father who cares about and loves my kids. They have a prominent place in my life and I will continue to have a close relationship with them."

To recap the theory:

| | |
|---|---|
| *Nurturing Parent:* | Shows caring and encourages growth |
| *Critical Parent:* | Is demanding, overbearing, critical |
| *Adult:* | Deals with reality, respects self/others |
| *Natural Child:* | Is fun to be with, honest, transparent |
| *Adapted Child:* | Is overrebellious or overcompliant |

In healthy communication, we use the *Nurturing Parent*, the *Adult*, and the *Natural Child*. The other parts are negative and produce problems in interaction.

## Interrogation Versus Inquiry

In separation/divorce, there are many issues that must be addressed. Matters regarding children, house, furniture, and child and spousal support are a few of the major problems needing negotiation. It is imperative to deal with a former spouse in ways that will work.

The most basic way we express thoughts is through words. The way we put them together determines how effective we will be as communicators. Our words have a great effect on relationships.

The premise in journalism is to ask, "Why, when, who, where, what, and how." As children we learn to ask questions—lots of them. It becomes ingrained in us. That is how most of us communicate.

In graduate school for my master's degree in counseling, one of the fundamental principles and demands was, "Don't ask questions." I couldn't believe it. I shone as a question asker. "There's no way I can keep from questioning," I reasoned. However, in the ensuing years, I have practiced this technique. It has become a natural flow for me, particularly when working as a therapist.

Whenever we employ the technique of questioning, it may be interpreted as interrogation. We are in control when we ask a lot of questions, for the person answering may be uncomfortable and tell things that are private. It is as though he has a hook in his mouth and is being pulled along by us. He may feel controlled and manipulated. An example would be:

> *Inquirer:* "Are you divorced?"
> *Person:* "Yes."
> *Inquirer:* "Well, whose fault was it? Did you want it? What did you do to deserve it? Have you given it much thought? Have you prayed about it?"

This an extreme example to illustrate how questions can be leading and controlling. Rather than ask a question, we might say, "Tell me about it." For example:

> *Inquirer:* "I understand you're divorced. Tell me about it."

At this point, the person has a right to say, "Oh, there isn't much to tell," and leave it, or he may go into great detail for twenty minutes. He has the option to tell as much or as little as he chooses. It comes down to respect for the person's right to be in control of what he shares.

When questions are used, many times we get only yes-and-no answers. It is quite obvious the person isn't willing to share.

## "I" Versus "You" Messages

When someone says, "You always . . . you never . . . you should . . . why don't you ever . . . ," our wall of defense goes up. Then, as soon as the person takes a breath, we jump in with reasons to justify ourselves. We may also tell specific areas in which the other person needs to improve! That is a "You message," and it is usually taken as blaming.

In contrast, an "I message" is honest, forthright, and does not accuse. It only states what we are thinking or feeling. For instance: "I was embarrassed the other day when you mentioned my divorce in front of a group of people. I would have preferred telling them myself at a future time when I felt more comfortable."

Very likely the person will respond, "You know, I guess I really did humiliate you, and I didn't mean it that way. I'm concerned about you and just wanted to share. I'm sorry."

Let's look at a divorcing couple:

*Husband:* "You witch! You just had to tell my parents about our split, didn't you? You can never keep your trap shut. I told you I wanted to tell them, but there you went, mouthing off. You make me sick!"

*Wife:* "Well, if you were any kind of a man, I wouldn't have to tell them. That's your problem—

you're a weasel, a wimp. You've always been one and
you'll be one 'til you die. You just can't face reality.''

And, the fight is on.

Consider a couple facing the same situation using ''I messages'' rather than ''You messages.''

*Husband:* ''I am really angry you told my parents
about our divorce. It's bad enough that it's happening,
but not hearing it from me makes it even worse for my
folks. I told you it was my responsibility and I would
do it.''

*Wife:* ''I don't blame you for being angry. I've been so
hurt that I really wanted to get back at you through
your family. Maybe we can't change what is happening to us, but we can be civil and stay away from the
low blows. I'm going to try.''

Now they have provided a healthy arena to talk out their
thoughts and feelings. When we do not feel the need to defend,
we are more able to be vulnerable in our truthfulness.

Using an ''I message'' is a good example of two people working out a difference while in their *Adult* ego state.

## Broken Record

Communication with a former spouse can be very difficult.
The couple often becomes sidetracked into emotional territory.

When speaking to a former mate, if phrases such as, ''Well, I
don't know,'' ''Maybe,'' or ''I guess so'' are consistent in your

end of the conversation, you are wide open to being shot down, disrespected, or manipulated.

> *Passive Mate:* "I was just wondering if maybe we could talk about the kids, if you want. If that's not okay, it's fine with me. I guess we could just try a little harder to make things work."

Instead of these passive-sounding statements, say, "I have decided" or "I choose to. . . ." These are the words of a person who has good self-esteem, self-respect, and direction. This is the *Adult* transaction.

> *Confident Mate:* "I think it is damaging to the kids when you say you will pick them up for the weekend and then don't show up. I choose to no longer look into their sad, disappointed eyes and make excuses for you. Only when I receive your telephone call stating that you are on the way will I tell the children and get them ready to go."

Sometimes there is continual blame and harassment. It is quite easy then to be sucked into an argument. Rather than a heated back-and-forth exchange, using the concept of a "Broken Record" breaks the destructive cycle. This excellent theory was created by Manuel J. Smith and used in his book *When I Say No I Feel Guilty.*

The Broken Record consists of repeating one small phrase over and over. The speaker stays with the issue, refusing to be side-tracked.

In therapy, Christopher blurted, "My wife wants to visit her parents in Oregon on a four-day weekend. I don't want to go.

"I have never felt accepted by her parents. The standard procedure for our visits is that my wife and the kids are with her mom and I'm stuck with her dad, who doesn't want me around. I'm tired of the whole mess. Even more, I am sick to death of pretending everything is okay."

We talked about the Broken Record concept and did some role playing.

The next time I saw Chris, he stated, "After my wife brought up the subject several times and wasn't listening to my answer, I decided to use the Broken Record theory. I said, 'I feel like a fifth wheel when I'm with your parents, and I choose not to go.' For five days, she continually brought it up, giving different arguments as to why I should go. Each time, my only response was, 'I feel like a fifth wheel, and I choose not to go.' I might have parroted this twenty or thirty times before my wife said, 'You really aren't going, are you?' I said, 'Right!'

"They all went to Oregon and had a wonderful weekend—so did I!"

By using the Broken Record, you keep to the subject and do not give reasons or answers. Eventually, you get through. I heartily advocate this theory to parents of teens, to clients in private therapy, and in workshops I teach. Over and over I hear the good results that occur when it is consistently used.

Communication, especially with a former spouse, is never easy. However, these ideas will bring improvement.

The benefits will be yours.

# Insight for Growth

1. It is very difficult to let go. "If I let go," you say, "there's nothing left. I can't deal with having nothing." But holding on sabotages growth. Name one thing you won't release that is deterring healing.

2. What would happen if you let it go? Write down some steps you could take to detach.

3. Decide in what part of the *Parent*, *Adult*, or *Child* you tend to operate.

|  | Often | Some | Seldom |
|---|---|---|---|
| *Critical Parent* | | | |
| *Nurturing Parent* | | | |
| *Adult* | | | |
| *Natural Child* | | | |
| *Adapted Child* (*Rebellious*) | | | |
| (*Compliant*) | | | |

4. Practice: "I message" and "Tell me"

# 4

# LEARNING TO BE REAL

His scrubbed, innocent face looked like that of an angel. As a smile danced across his face, his eyes lit up like tiny firecrackers exploding on a sultry July night.

It was hard to believe he was in prison.

For more than three years, I counseled incarcerated teenage "men." Not boys—men. Men who had not been protected, guided, and nurtured. As young boys, they were turned loose on the streets to fend for themselves.

After working with hundreds of inmates, I learned some things about the criminal mind: how to better protect myself from being taken advantage of, insight into the thinking process of the male, and how to spot a liar. On occasion, a counselor would wonder aloud if a lad was telling the truth. A co-worker's reply might be, "Was his mouth moving? If it was, he was lying." Often, this response was not too farfetched.

Even though I was empathetic, caring, and a good listener, on occasion I bombarded these youths with truth. Only when there was truth between us could mentally healthy attitudes germinate and grow. I am convinced that a life of honesty is one of the foundations of happiness and self-fulfillment.

As a child, I was raised with a sense of honesty. Lying was considered a horrid thing. On the few occasions when I have lied, my guilt has overwhelmed me and I've made the matter right. I continue to feel strongly about truth. Conversely, when someone lies to me, I am livid with rage.

Even though I didn't tell outright lies, on examination I found my life was basically one of deception. My dishonesty came to the fore in an unwillingness to tell how I really felt and in going along with the program. I also lied to myself about my anger and pretended it wasn't there. Soon I was no longer aware of its existence. I lived a passive existence in my *Compliant Child*. My self-esteem was low. Not feeling I deserved to be respected, I allowed people to walk all over me while I kept silent. Only after the breakup of my marriage did I begin to see the pathology of my life-style.

There are three positions in which to conduct interpersonal communication: passive, aggressive, or assertive.

Learning to tell the truth about feelings and thoughts in a kind, assertive manner has been a laborious exercise in growth, yet one that has freed me and enriched my life.

## Passive/Aggressive/Assertive

A few years back, Assertiveness Training seminars were all the rage. Some were called Sensitivity Training. People sat in a circle and, in their honest appraisal, ripped the self-worth of others to shreds. How destructive.

Yet there is a need to be assertive to build a good self-worth and grow toward a positive life-style.

According to Thomas A. Harris, in his book *I'm O.K.—You're O.K.*, there are three positions. Each has a unique philosophy:

| | |
|---|---|
| Passive: | "You win, I lose" |
| Aggressive: | "I win, you lose" |
| Assertive: | "I win, you win" |

Being assertive means I will not trample over you but I will not allow you to disrespect me. If you do, in a quiet yet strong way, I will confront you.

To illustrate: As I was easing my cart into the supermarket checkout line, I spied a woman coming toward me. With hair flying, purse swinging wildly from her arm, feet galloping on the tiled floor, she had a death grasp on her basket as she shoved it in front of mine.

Being a *passive* person, my reaction was to allow her to invade my territory. Anger began to well inside me. *What a first-class jerk*, I thought. The angry feelings were reflected in my sour face as I checked out and drove home. To further express how I felt, I cut off two people in traffic and was mad for hours. I lost, she won.

Being an *aggressive* person was more enticing. With erupting rage, I grabbed the basket, slung it, and watched the groceries fly and crash land, tumbling over the floor in a broken, sloppy mess. As the clerk and customers watched in amazement and horror, I continued the rampage by declaring (in choice, loud language) what I thought of her barging into my space. I won, she lost.

(Actually, I chose to be neither passive nor aggressive. Instead, I decided to be *assertive*.)

Since I had been learning about assertiveness, I thought now would be a good time to practice. Tapping the woman on the shoulder, I smiled and said, "Excuse me, but I was in front of you." Looking surprised, she mused, "Oh, I'm sorry," and proceeded to pull her cart behind mine. We then chatted about the weather as we checked out. We both seemed comfortable. I had dealt with my anger in a positive way and could let it go.

I won, she won.

You are probably thinking, *Yeah, what if she hadn't moved?* I would have gently pushed her basket behind mine as I quietly and firmly stated, "I'm sorry, but I was in front of you."

When we practice kind confrontation, most of the time we can live in an assertive mode. We begin to feel better about ourselves and others. We no longer need to pretend we are not angry but can honestly deal with the problem.

For many, learning to be assertive takes a pendulum swing from passive to aggressive. It takes time to back down from aggression and find the midpoint (assertive position).

For me, one indication of aggressiveness is when my voice gets loud. I'm striving to back down and confront in a caring, honest manner.

Most of my life I was a passive person. I stuffed my anger inside. Sometimes I told others about it rather than face the individual concerned. Most of the time I pretended it didn't matter, it didn't hurt, or I wasn't mad.

Recently I have crossed the line. Now, I am most uncomfortable with passive behavior. It is more satisfying to confront the issue with the person involved and work out the problem. Only then can I let it go.

In confrontation, it is important to use an "I message" so the person will not feel blamed and we can work out our differences.

A man who works in a lesser position than me was angry at something I had done. Rather than come to me, he went to the "top brass." My superior and I discussed the problem and found it was a wrong assumption. We came to an amicable solution.

But I could not let it go. As the episode continually wormed its way into my thoughts, I was anxious and irritated. The more I tried to stuff it down and pretend it didn't matter, the more it cropped up.

Hurrying through the office one morning, I saw my co-worker. *Oh, well,* I thought, *that's life—forget it. No!* I decided. *There you go again—being passive, pretending, avoiding confrontation. Get over there and settle it.*

Gritting my teeth, I edged over to him. "Jess, could I talk with you a minute?" He nodded affirmation. Swallowing, I continued, "We've always worked well together and I want it to continue. I was bothered because you talked to Mr. Jones before me. I would have liked the opportunity to work it out with you. Then, if you weren't satisfied, I would have had no problem with your going to Mr. Jones. I felt bad that you didn't approach me first."

Looking stunned, Jess said, "I'm sorry. You're my friend, and next time I'll come to you first." We resolved the issue.

If I had been unwilling to confront Jess, a nagging uncomfortableness and mistrust would have permeated my relationship with him. Now we are free to be compatible co-workers.

## Self-Esteem

My definition of healthy self-esteem is this: an honest evaluation of oneself—not exaggerated or underrated. The more honest we are, the more free to be ourselves and grow.

As with most divorced people, it was so easy for me to place full blame on my former husband for the divorce. However, I had to come to the realization that my life also needed some drastic changes. During the separation/divorce, I realized there was a choice—to end up either bitter or better. Looking myself squarely in the face, I said, "I'll be darned if I'm going through all this for nothing. When this is over, I want to be a healthy person."

Often we want our former spouse to transform, and we think, *God knows he/she needs it!* But we are responsible *only* for ourselves. If we do not change, we will attract the same type of person and go through it all over again.

"I'm in love," the divorced man oozed. "She's just wonderful. In only two weeks, we were sure. There's no need to wait. We want to get married now."

And they did.

And they divorced.

But not until enormous pain had eroded the marriage, a baby boy was born, and they were financially bankrupt. The union had become a living hell.

Because neither person was willing to work on individual issues, to grow, to allow time to heal, each of them married a person similar to the former spouse. They were fooled by external appearances—different colored eyes and hair. The insides were the same.

It is tempting to blame everything on the divorce and abdicate responsibility for growth, but when we are honest, we begin to see some deplorable personality flaws. It is difficult to be candid because it brings us to a choice: to grow (which is a lot of hard work) or to continue a dishonest life-style. Breaking bad habits and changing attitudes takes courage.

In my private practice, I give personality tests to clients. Because I rather enjoy test taking and learning new things about myself, I take the tests first.

As I answered the questions on one test, they became tedious.

"They're asking the same dumb questions over and over," I fumed. "This is really a stupid test." Exasperated, I plowed through.

When I scored the exam, my rebellion surfaced. "Rebellious?" I spewed. "This was one of the most inane tests I've taken. What do they know? It's totally unreliable."

In the ensuing days, my brain flashed back to episodes, situations, and responses that illustrated my rebellious spirit. Trying to shove it down became disconcerting and then impossible.

It took several days before I would admit the results were accurate. Defiance was a part of me I didn't like. But once I acknowledged it, I began working toward change.

## Developing a Good Self-Image

Let's look at three ways to attain a healthy estimation of ourselves: Freedom of Choice, Resisting Negative Affirmations, and Stress Management.

First, we have the *freedom of choice* in regard to a good self-worth. We can make selections that will either contribute to it or tear it down. In fact, we have great control over most of our lives by the decisions we make.

When we make good choices, we reap good consequences. Thus, the possibilities are nearly unlimited for a satisfying life. The decisions that bring about change begin in our thought process.

Conversely, the more negative our thinking, the worse our lives. It takes constant and consistent practice to reverse a negative mind-set.

I believe there are three steps to making significant life changes. First, make a logical decision. Second, execute behavior that correlates to the decision. Third, feelings will follow.

Let's say a person hates his job. He has dreaded going to work for years. Because he doesn't feel like making a change, he handles it by constant complaining. In order to deal with the situation in a positive way, he first must make a decision.

*Logical Decision.* "I've been in this dead-end occupation for thirteen years. It's driving me crazy and enough is enough. I will actively pursue a change by looking for another job. My goal is to have a position I will enjoy and am qualified for in six months."

*Behavior:* He now must correlate his behavior with his decision: look in the classified ads, mention it to friends, meet with an employment agency representative, write and mail resumés, talk to others in the field, take a Kuder Interest Survey (to assess skills), call a "headhunter," fill out applications, explore the philosophies of different companies, research positions and the expected growth of corporations, and go on interviews.

*Feelings:* As the behavior is executed, feelings will become more positive, as will attitude. The job hunter will begin to feel this was a good decision. *Feelings* will catch up with the original *decision*. Before long, he will be in a job he enjoys and will wonder why he waited so long to change.

Yet, often it is the reverse. We do not step out or risk because we are waiting to feel like it. Frankly, we will probably never feel like it. Thus, life may become boring and stagnant even though it is effortless. The zip is gone. It is a passive existence.

When we move forward based on a logical decision that has been well thought out and researched, life becomes good. It is palatable because we are more in control.

It is easier, and sometimes quite desirable, to want circumstances to manage our lives. It is the path of least resistance. We then become victimized by our own passivity. Nothing good ever happens, and things we don't like occur. Life is out of control.

Proverbs 16:9 RSV states, "A man's mind plans his way, but the Lord directs his steps." This suggests to me that we need to get off our backsides. God directs our walking, not sitting. Seldom do we get guidance when we are on the sofa. It comes when we are doing, walking, moving. We can't expect God to open a door when we are too lazy or timid to knock.

We have great input into our lives when we make good decisions and follow through with action. It takes guts. The outcome is mentally healthy.

In counseling hundreds of separated/divorced people, I sense many would rather whine and complain about their lot in life than to do something positive to stimulate change. So, the protests drone on for years like broken records—as do their lives. They can't understand why nothing gets better.

People who have taken the bull by the horns and directed their lives heal more quickly and acquire more positive life-styles. Also, they are happier.

One Sunday afternoon I was prostrate on the floor, in the depths of despair. I had been crying for hours. I was feeling sorry for myself and enjoying it (in a neurotic sense). A thought bombarded me: *What a jerk you are, Jeenie, lying here crying your eyes out for someone who could care less. When are you going to get your act together? You're disgusting!*

*Hmmmm*, the logical part of me responded. *This is crazy,* my thoughts continued. *I've wasted my afternoon having a pity party. How ridiculous.*

I jumped up, looked in the newspaper for a movie, washed my face, did a new makeup job, and was out of the house in fifteen minutes. Walking jauntily to the ticket window, I secured my pass, a tub of popcorn, and sauntered into the theater. The picture was light, hilarious, and exactly what I needed. I giggled, screamed, clapped, roared, and held my stomach. I went home refreshed, renewed, revitalized.

Rather than choose defeat and despair, I decided to take charge of my life. Because my alternative was good, so were the results. The decision to stop my pity party led to behavior change (going to see an enjoyable movie), and positive feelings followed.

When life is based on feelings, we live on a roller coaster emotional ride—up one day (or minute), down the next. Our lives are controlled by outside sources. We remain in a spectator position, tossed and whirled around by whatever blows by. We feel depressed, hopeless, and stuck.

Only when we decide to get in the driver's seat and steer our own lives do we find control and contentment.

Choosing the course of our lives is not always fun, however, for we are then responsible for the consequences of our decisions. We can't place blame. For this reason, it is easier to let others or circumstances control us. Then there is always a villain. We get off the hook. But we lose our human value.

Second, in developing good self-worth, it is vital to *resist negative affirmations*—stop knocking ourselves. Learning to graciously accept a compliment and respond with a simple "thank you" is an important part of the process.

A young man who is a dear friend of mine drives me crazy. He is multitalented, handsome, and intelligent. Yet he cannot accept a compliment. Gourmet cooking is among his accomplishments. At a dinner party, the commendations roll, and they are deserved. His response is, "I can't believe the roast is so dry. This darned Jell-O didn't set the way it should. The dessert looked beautiful in the picture, and how I could have messed it up is beyond me."

It becomes a contest. Whatever praise is given, he is one ahead in pointing out imperfections. This negativism has infected his life-style. He believes nothing is ever good enough, and he lets everyone know all the boring details.

Soon, people withhold sincere tribute.

Then there are those who spiritualize compliments. When someone says, "I really appreciated your solo. You have a lovely voice," the musician responds with a godly, "It's not me. I'm nothing. It's the Lord, and He deserves all the credit."

Come on. The soloist has spent hours practicing, paid money for private lessons, given up activities to perfect the craft. There has been an investment of time and energy. I really don't think God would be displeased if the person merely responded with a sincere, "Thank you."

It takes practice to discontinue putting ourselves down verbally. The process begins in our thoughts, and it takes constant effort to stop the flow of negative input.

When I realize I'm into a negative thought pattern, I say aloud, "Stop it, Jeenie!" Then I deliberately turn my mind to something more positive. Often this needs to be done hundreds of times daily. Eventually, the destructive thoughts are less frequent and last a shorter period of time.

Since everyone has numerous areas of weakness, it is easy to accentuate and dwell on them. But it is very damaging. It is vital to *emphasize* our *strengths* and encourage ourselves to be all we can be.

I am not advocating ignoring or not working on our negative side. However, it is essential to not make it a main emphasis in life. The more self-nurturing we are, the more positive will be our outlook on life.

Third, *stress management* is fundamental to a good mental

image, which propels us toward a productive life-style. Hans Selye, who began major work in the field, suggested that a grateful heart is a key stress reliever. I concur. The more thankful and noncomplaining we are, the happier and less stressful we become. In another chapter, I will discuss this topic in detail.

## Honesty in Parenting

Single parents have a different set of problems. Many of them try to be both father and mother. It becomes all-consuming and unrealistic.

It is crucial to be the best mother *or* father we can but not try to make up for the loss of the other parent. The children will be happier and feel more secure.

Honesty about the divorce is imperative, and the details need to vary according to the ages of the children. A rule of thumb is to forthrightly tell them only what they ask—no more. When they are ready for additional information, they will inquire.

Ten years after my divorce, my daughter and I had a long, gut-level talk. We had previously conversed at various times, but only at the level of query. On this occasion, it was total honesty, at her request. At one point, feeling a bit uncomfortable, I asked, "Kathi, are you sure you want to know all this?" With her affirmation, we continued. She knew far more than I had supposed, yet I felt good about not having divulged unsolicited information over the years. The right timing ultimately occurred, but it took a decade.

It is very difficult to keep a closed mouth regarding the child's other parent. Even though I tried to keep quiet, there were times I made unkind remarks about my former husband and, on occasion, stooped to interrogation when my daughter returned from visitation. It was wrong.

Yet, I honestly tried to encourage my daughter to respect and love her father, for I have a great sense of responsibility to God to help my child honor her dad. Even though this is my desire, often I've failed miserably.

Storming into my office, eyes ablaze and body rigid with emotion, a man dragged three small children behind him and bounced them on to the sofa. With a barrage of cursing, he berated the children's mother. Tears made narrow pathways down their pink little cheeks, and tiny shoulders shook with sobs as these precious children heard words that cut into their tender hearts.

The father spoke truth, but such detailed honesty was inappropriate for little ears. It was too intense, too overwhelming. My heart went out to all of them in their suffering, yet I was angry at the father's inconsiderateness.

Only years will tell the deep damage inflicted, not only by the mother leaving but also by the insensitivity of the father in "telling all."

In time, children generally see through the marital problems and come to their own conclusions. They are then free to love and respect each parent in a more honest, wholesome way.

An honest life-style sets us free to be assertive, admit our failures and successes, have a healthy self-image, and pursue the intimacies of good relationships.

What better advice than this from Jesus: "And you shall know the truth, and the truth shall make you free"(John 8:32 NAS).

# Insight for Growth

1. Being real is scary. It makes a person vulnerable to hurt, disappointment, and pain. But its reward is freedom. In what mode do you most often communicate?

|            | Often | Some | Seldom |
|------------|-------|------|--------|
| Passive    |       |      |        |
| Aggressive |       |      |        |
| Assertive  |       |      |        |

2. Think of an incident in which you acted either in a passive or aggressive way. Decide how it could have been done assertively. Write the dialogue.

3. What two things are holding you back from having a more healthy self-esteem?

4. Choose a method that will help you change.

# 5

# GETTING ON WITH LIFE

Some people watch things happen, others make things happen, and still others don't know what's happening! Making things happen takes a lot of discipline, a willingness to give up other activities, and much perseverance. It's just plain hard work. Frankly, at this moment, I would rather be lying on the sofa watching TV!

After learning of my husband's dissatisfaction, which led to the eventual dissolution of our marriage, I was faced with an uncertain future. Fear gripped me in a stranglehold. Breathing became labored and emotional pain shot through my veins like a lethal dosage.

Years earlier, I had completed three years of college, dropped out, and worked full-time so my husband could complete undergraduate and graduate degrees. Following the completion of his education, I chose to work part-time in a church secretarial/treasurer position in order to be at home when my husband and daughter left and returned. Providing a haven for them was a priority.

After the truth set in, my mind kept screaming, *I did it all for nothing—sacrificed, cared, gave—for nothing.* My thoughts overwhelmed my emotions and logic.

My mother had died many years earlier, but she left me an unspoken legacy: "When things are really bad, allow for grief, then get up and do something about it." I followed her sage advice.

*I can't let this destroy me,* I thought. *I've got to get myself together and do something. It will take guts, grit, and truckloads of determination, but I will survive.*

So, traveling an hour to my alma mater, I had my transcript evaluated. It was my only hope. God sent a compassionate registrar to guide me with a plan to complete the nearly one year remaining to earn a B.A. degree. However, I had missed the registration deadline for the semester. The rule at this Christian college stated that the last twenty-four units must be taken on campus. He waived it and suggested I take a quarter at the state university, which he would accept.

Calling the state university, I found classes would begin the following week. After filling out the required forms, I gingerly went to the registration desk. "I'm really desperate," I told the clerk. "Is there any way I can process the application to begin classes?"

"Lady," she yawned, "the only way this could happen is for you to walk the application through, and that's impossible."

Proverbs 16:9 NAS says, "The mind of man plans his way, But the Lord directs his steps." *Well,* I thought, *I've gotten off my derriere, made plans, and now it's time to start walking. As I do, God will divinely direct.*

Cocking my head, with a sparkle in my eye, I questioned, "Which office is first?" She pointed. With an air of importance and confidence, I went from person to person. Rubber stamps slammed down on the document and puzzled looks crossed faces, but the application was processed.

The October sun was brilliant and cheery, matching my disposition, as I got all dressed up in my school clothes for my first day. The drive was beautiful. The parking lot was a mess. Even trudging from the far end of the campus coin lot (it was cheaper) didn't dampen my spirits. Looking at the enormity of the campus and buildings took an edge off my enthusiasm, but I managed to spot the engineering building and was whisked by elevator to the top floor.

With fervor, I threw open the door of my first class in statistics. Looking around the room, I found it packed with young, aspiring, bored engineers. The professor stopped talking as I nervously tried to find a place. In the center of the room was a lone seat. Creeping down the aisle, as all eyes watched, I shyly slid into the desk.

Breathing a sigh of relief, I turned my attention to the lecture. But something was wrong. I didn't feel comfortable and no amount of adjusting lessened the feeling. In assessing the problem, I realized I had entered the seat the wrong way. In my anxiety, I got in from the right side, scooting between the desk arm and the back of the seat. No wonder it felt strange. My legs were hanging over a bar to the right, and it was too high to bring them over to the proper position.

I considered my options: I could get up, go to the front of the room, walk down the correct side of the aisle, and be seated. Or I could stay where I was.

Going to the front of the room and back around would let

everyone in the room know I was a semi-idiot. If I stayed where I was, only the few around me would know. After careful calculation, I chose the latter.

Listening to the lecture on statistics, I was overwhelmed with confusion. My math skills were limited, and the student engineers around me were yawning from boredom, having been through calculus. My legs went to sleep. I concluded something had to be done. Carefully I grabbed one leg and eased it over the bar and on to the floor. "Hmmm, that's better," I sighed. Now I was sitting in a straddled position. *No problem*, I thought, *I can handle it.*

Moments later, stress took over. *This is driving me crazy,* my emotions screamed. Then logic kicked in. *If I could get one leg over the bar, I'm certainly capable of managing the other one. Sounds like a plan,* I thought. Cautiously grabbing my right leg, I gently began pulling it over. As I did, my desk began to tip toward the floor.

I could envision the desk sliding, careening over the waxed title, books flying upward, gliding along the aisle, smashing into human legs, papers fluttering through space from the opened spiral rings of the notebook, pencils whizzing through the air, and me flat on my back, legs ceilingward, with a look of horror and foolishness on my face.

This was not a pretty picture. So, pushing my leg back over the bar, I remained suspended through the remainder of the class. Waiting until the room cleared, I climbed out of my predicament and sped out the door.

I dropped the class.

However, in May I graduated with a B.A. degree and began a master's degree in counseling. (P.S. At the master's level, I again took statistics and earned an *A*). Near the end of the program, my husband left me.

Had these traumatic events not occurred in my life, I would have continued in a complacent life-style. Because of my circumstances, I was forced to set some goals. Panic gave me reason to reevaluate, plan, and strive for new vistas.

It is amazing to think what can be accomplished by first, deciding on a goal; second, establishing steps toward its accomplishment; and third, working the plan.

If we work our plan daily, the days soon roll into weeks, then into months, and finally years. We experience the joys of dreams fulfilled.

## The Process

Decide on a goal. It must be realistic, reachable, and measurable. Perhaps you have not been goal oriented. If so, make it simple.

Think through the time needed for completion, and set a date. A due date helps to keep us on track. If the completion date is in a year, break down what needs to be done monthly and write it on a calendar. Then list weekly and daily steps.

When we do a small amount daily, it is more possible to reach our goal by the completion date. It is sometimes tempting to be unrealistic in our enthusiasm and plan far more than is probable. This results in discouragement.

Again, the goal must be realistic and reachable.

Picture a pole vaulter. He begins to train for the sport by placing the bar in a low position, one that is realistic and attainable. He doggedly practices and eventually scales the bar. After he has accomplished that height, he raises the bar. Again, he continues to work until he soars over the bar. He continues the process and one day reaches heights he never thought possible.

So in life, we set the bar (in terms of goals) and continually try. However, when we are "inches" away from attaining our goal, we *raise the bar*. Our striving then becomes self-defeating. We say such things as, "I just can't believe it. I try and try, but nothing ever works out for me. The more I try, the worse it gets. It's just no use."

The real problem is we have not given ourselves permission to be successful. We keep raising the bar in an effort to sabotage our efforts. It works. Just before we can enjoy some of the fruits of our labor, we mess it up. We fail—again.

The pole vaulter raises the bar *only* after he has successfully attained the new height. He has experienced the exhilaration of having won. He enjoys his moment of glory. Then, and only then, does he raise the bar.

We, too, need to allow ourselves the joy of attainment. It is okay to be happy, to feel proud of our accomplishments, to be pleased with our efforts. If we raise the bar prior to having met our goal, it might mean we are afraid of success, or conversely, that we have a fear of failure.

It is all right to place the bar (goal) at a very low level so that you can be successful. After the goal is attained, enjoy it. Revel in the excitement and contentment. Then set a higher goal.

## Fear of Failure

My master's program was very intense. Often I walked to my car late at night thinking, *Jeenie, give it up. You're out of your league. These people are smart. You're not of the same caliber. You're wasting your time and effort.*

Part of our monthly examinations included submitting two video and three audiotapes of counseling sessions. It entailed about twenty hours of intense preparatory work. A number of times, I submitted five tapes and only one or two of them were considered adequate to pass. I was discouraged. I later learned many students dropped out of the program because of its difficulty and leaning toward failure orientation. But I stayed.

The Abnormal Psychology course was extraordinarily demanding. I taped the class and memorized a great deal of the lectures. For the written exam, I gave not only my interpretation but quoted the professor verbatim as well. Even so, I was unable to give him what he wanted. I failed the course. No one fails a class at a master's level. It is unheard of. Somehow I managed to do the impossible.

Later I learned that most of the other students were having similar struggles. At the end of the program, comprehensive exams were given for all of the course work. It was mandatory that we again pass former classes at a *B* letter grade or better. People were so distraught they were sick in the bathrooms. Aspirin was popped like candy. Nerves were ragged.

Many evenings I was in a state of depression. I felt I was not intellectually capable and was very unwise to continue degrading myself. But because I had seen God open the doors for this program, I was determined to continue, regardless. I retook the Abnormal Psychology course, passed it, and earned my M.S. degree.

Thus, one of the great lessons of my life was learned: *I can fail yet succeed*! Even though I was unable to pass a class and some exams, I still attained the ultimate goal of a master's degree. In retrospect, this experience became an area of growth and freed me to continue in the face of failure. What a lesson.

We will always experience anxiety in new circumstances, but taking the immobilizing fear out of failure gives us the courage to dream our dreams and work toward their fulfillment.

## Marking Time

It is easy to sit and mark time, waiting for something wonderful to happen—the "right job" or the "right spouse." We almost get sofa sores. There is, however, a choice. We can be pioneers or settlers.

History books are full of enchanting stories of pioneers. In the Old West, a pioneer jumped on his horse, got going, and blazed trails. There was danger, excitement, and achievement. The settler sat.

Yvonne was divorced and working as a housekeeper but dreamed of being a legal secretary. After hearing hours of complaining, I suggested she take a course at the local community college. "It will entail two evenings per week, but in about two years, you'll have an A.A. degree and be prepared for the career you want," I said.

Her face contorted as she sighed, "Two nights a week. I can't spend two nights a week in class. I want to be home every night."

She is still home, working in a job she hates and complaining to everyone who walks by. She settled instead of soared.

Conversely, as I was completing my master's degree, my brother-in-law remarked to me, "I've always wanted one, too. But it would take me two years and I'd be almost forty years old." To which I replied, "How old will you be in two years anyway?" He answered, "Forty."

It spurred him to enroll and complete a master's program,

finishing just prior to his fortieth birthday. "Many times it was tough," he said. "I left work tired, hungry, and in no mood for class. The hours of grueling study and writing volumes of papers were tedious and exhausting. But your words continually came back to me and I was able to keep going."

He has since become a published author, heads up the Education Department at a Christian college, and has earned acclaim in his field and completed a doctorate!

## "Seeing" a Dream Come True

Everyone who is normal has fantasized. It can be a healthy and delightful pastime. It can also help us "see" where we would like to be in the future and strive toward it.

After I earned my master's degree, I began working on an M.F.C.C. (Marriage, Family, Child Counselor) license. This license required three thousand hours of volunteer counseling, an intense written examination, and a rigorous oral examination.

Even though I was working full-time as a high-school counselor, I could not claim the hours because there was no qualified supervisor on campus. My only option was to follow every lead for volunteer counseling and work on it little by little. Most of the ideas were dead ends, as were some of the supervisors, but I kept plugging away year after year even though I was often discouraged.

It took nearly ten years to collect enough hours.

Nervously, I walked into California State University at Long Beach to take the written exam. It seemed I had studied my brains dry. I had reviewed, learned new material, memorized, and sweated out nearly five months of preparation. Now I was ready.

Six weeks later, I fearfully removed an envelope from the

mailbox and read the results. I was horrified when I learned the outcome: I had missed a passing mark by two questions. "Unbelievable," I said aloud. "All that work for nothing. I failed." My overwhelming thought was, *Give up. Chuck this thing. It's not worth it.*

In a few days, I calmed down and logic took over. Since I could retake the exam in six months, I decided to go for it. After taking a two-week break, I again spent most of my free hours studying. Also, I began visualizing going to my mailbox and opening the letter that said, "Congratulations! Your Marriage, Family, Child Counseling license number is. . . ."

The second time around, I had devised a system for the exam. As I carefully read each question, I answered it before looking at the multiple choices. Once I answered, I did not go back to change it (as I had done previously). Even though I was not told my score, I feel confident I passed 100 percent.

The final step was to begin the exhausting six-month preparation for the oral examination.

The day dawned bright, the sky was vividly blue, and mounds of cottonlike clouds looked as though they had been thrown into the sky. Even a good night's sleep and a nutritious breakfast did not calm my fears as I drove into Los Angeles to U.S.C. for the oral exam.

Finding the examination site, I was escorted to the "holding tank" with thirty or so others. Sweaty palms, pounding hearts, and nervous smiles were the order of the day.

For years, I had listened to terrifying stories of the oral examination in front of the panel of experts who passed judgment. Thumbs up or thumbs down! Fates were sealed.

My panel was nearly an exact replica of the tales. One member was perhaps a bit worse. He badgered over and over until I felt weak. At one point, I sighed, "God, I need your help." Then I looked at the man and thought, *Okay, sucker, I've worked long and hard for this. I'm a good therapist and I am not going to fail.* Walking out of the room, I felt as if my energy had literally flowed out through my feet. I was so disoriented I could hardly find the elevator.

The long six-week wait for results began. Some days I was certain I'd passed; other times I was afraid I hadn't. But my decision was to take the oral exam again if I had failed. Still, I kept the picture of the congratulatory letter in my mind's eye.

"Congratulations! Your Marriage, Family, Child Counseling license number is . . ." sent me spinning, jumping, screaming, and thanking the Lord when the mailbox contained my anticipated letter. My prayers were answered. I had passed!

The brain is a marvelous mechanism. It cannot, however, distinguish between what is real and what is visualized. Thus, we can picture success in life while telling ourselves encouraging statements that will propel us toward our goals.

## Balance

Living in balance is desirable yet difficult to accomplish.

One way to achieve balance is to set yearly goals in six areas: Physical, Spiritual, Mental, Emotional, Financial, and Family. Each heading should contain no more than three goals. As an example:

| | |
|---|---|
| *Physical:* | 1. Exercise 3 times weekly (20+ minutes) |
| | 2. Lose 10 pounds |
| | 3. Eat nutritionally daily |
| *Spiritual:* | 1. Pray 5 minutes daily |
| | 2. Read 5 Bible verses daily |

| *Mental:* | 1. Read 1 book quarterly |
| | 2. Take 1 class |
| *Emotional:* | 1. Talk to a friend weekly |
| | 2. Use 1 hour weekly for recreation |
| *Financial:* | 1. Save $10.00 monthly |
| | 2. Invest $100.00 yearly in a mutual fund |
| *Family:* | 1. Talk to each child alone 5 minutes a day |
| | 2. Hug and touch each child daily |

Again, goals must be reachable and measurable. It is wise to display them so they can be read daily. The bathroom mirror is a super place. As they are continually reviewed, we begin to work toward accomplishing them. Daily we are aware of how we are doing and what adjustments need to be made.

At the end of the year, we can make a note beside the goal as to what percentage has been accomplished. Some may have been completed 100 percent, others 50 percent, and perhaps some were hardly started. Even though they may not all have been met, we are much further along than if we had not planned.

It is then time to begin a process of reevaluation and revision of goals for the coming year. Generally it is wise to do some brainstorming on paper, let the ideas sit for several weeks, then formalize goals for the forthcoming year.

As an example, one of my Emotional goals was to go to the beach monthly. Running along the sand, feeling the fresh, salty air swirl through my hair, listening to the ebb and flow of the waves, feeling the cool sand between my toes, and climbing out on the rocks and watching the breakers smash against them all have great therapeutic value for me. I especially enjoy the solitude of the off-season months. Returning home, I feel as though I can conquer the world. There is a sense of peace and happiness.

When I assessed this particular goal at the end of the year, I found I had gone to the beach twice. Going monthly was not realistic. The bar was placed too high. So I changed it to once a quarter for the new year. Oddly, during that year, I went nearly once a month.

> When I play, I play hard.
> When I work, I work hard.

This became a motto for me in college—one I still practice. For instance, if when I am playing I continually think about how I should be working, it ruins the fun, and vice versa. It is vital to have times of hard work as well as times of fun.

We read in Ecclesiastes, "There is an appointed time for everything. And there is a time for every event under heaven. . . . A time to plant, and a time to uproot what is planted. . . . A time to weep, and a time to laugh; A time to mourn, and a time to dance . . ." (3:1, 2, 4 NAS). The verse continues to beautifully illustrate the concept of balance. Since God has given this guideline, we have an obligation to obey by striving to bring symmetry into our lives.

Another way I bring equilibrium to life is by conducting each segment of my life as though I were switching a TV channel.

Thursday is a most hectic day for me. Bounding out of bed (at least *once* I actually bounded), I'm consumed with getting ready for the day. Putting my car in gear at 7:00 A.M., I begin to prepare my thoughts for the day as a full-time high school counselor. After a full day, I change to the therapist channel and head for my private practice, where I work with clients until after 10:00 P.M. Getting into my car, I turn the key in the ignition, enter my "kick back" mode, and let the drama of the day dissipate into yawns and engulfing quietness.

Continually, and for each distinct aspect of my life, I switch. It helps me to be more fully at work (or play) without as much interference or contamination from other parts of life. Each division of life is more satisfying because I am really "tuned in."

To truly maximize our lives, we need a plan and the perseverance to implement it on a daily basis. A phrase I like is, "Shoot at nothing and you will hit it!" As long as we are shooting, let's take good aim and make it count.

# Insight for Growth

1. Separation/divorce is so difficult. It takes the joy from life and slaps us into a "don't care" mode. Not much looks good anymore, and it won't unless we *decide* to make life count. Think through a one-year goal in each of these areas and write it down:

   Physical:

   Spiritual:

   Mental:

   Emotional:

   Financial:

   Family:

2. In five years, the horrid ache will be gone. You will be healed. Look ahead now. Write down *exactly* who you want to be and what you want to have accomplished in five years.

3. Write down the first step toward that goal.

# 6

# FORGIVENESS: THE PATH TO FREEDOM

Gary cocked his head and wrinkled his brow as the impact of my counsel began to slowly sink in. When the realization was born, his jaw stiffened, red veins popped up in his neck, and the color etched its way through his face and toward the top of his head. "You're asking me to forgive that no-good wife for dumping me, ripping out my guts, treating me like garbage? Come on! There is *no way* I am going to forgive and forget this. Never!"

His statement sounds as if forgiveness benefits only the other person. No, forgiveness benefits *us*. It cleanses us and gives us a new chance to live and love again. It is freedom.

But, oh, how difficult to face it—to give up our right to revenge. It seems so unfair. We have been misused and devalued. It feels as if life is over. How overwhelming to even think of needing to forgive.

Sitting by the bedside of Corrie ten Boom one spring day, I listened to her stories and saw the excitement dance across her face as she described the new book she was writing. Her voice was vibrant and alive, her personality charming. Splashed across her face in vivid colors was a pictorial portrayal of peace, contentment, love of life.

Miss ten Boom was a victim of Hitler's inhumanity during World War II. She lived through the horrors of a concentration camp. Years later, she came face-to-face with the Nazi guard who had perpetrated the atrocities of war on her. Forgiveness was a struggle, yet she chose to obey her Lord.

As I looked at the tender, tranquil face of Corrie, I caught a firsthand glimpse of the rewards of forgiveness.

Forgiveness is a new topic that is being written about and encouraged by therapists. It is amazing that it has taken thousands of years for the concept to hit the psychological circles. The Bible is full of admonitions regarding forgiveness and its healing effect. This truth has finally made its mark on our modern-day thinkers.

As a therapist, I confront the issue of forgiveness with clients. Divorcing people have deep hurts. They often deal not only with the divorce issues but also with deep childhood trauma that may have been repressed. A great number of people were abused as children. The violation may have been physical, emotional, verbal, or sexual. Often it is a combination.

Because victims tend to behave in dysfunctional ways, marriage problems can be an outgrowth. For instance, victims will stay in marriages where there is flagrant infidelity, physical and emotional abuse, alcoholism, and drug addiction because they do not feel they are valuable enough to expect anything better. The divorced person needs to face the mistreatment and eventually forgive the perpetrator as well as himself for his inability to do anything differently. That is when healing and wholeness come.

As healing is a process, so is forgiveness. We would like it to be instantaneous, but it is not. Even the onset is gradual. One day we come to the realization that it is complete.

There are several stages of forgiveness:

## Stage One: Admission of Pain

So much of the time when we have been hurt, we want to pretend it isn't so. It is embarrassing to admit that someone had so much control over our feelings, that we had a deep need for the person, or that the relationship evidently meant more to us than to him or her. It is extremely difficult to admit pain and even harder to confront the person with our feelings, but as long as we pretend, we can never reach the point of forgiveness.

Even though I am gradually learning to admit and express my anger, it is still quite difficult for me to say, "My feelings have been hurt, and I need to talk to you about it." It is important that pain be faced in an honest manner, yet in order to appear strong and get through the process quickly, some people pretend it really doesn't matter. In reality, they feel as if they have been torn apart. Admitting the enormity of the anguish to oneself and to others is vital.

## Stage Two: Anger

Anger is a valid emotion. When we have been violated, it angers us. We have rightful cause to be mad. Anger, however, can be destructive or constructive.

A passive person may internalize fury. He or she may pretend it is not there or justify the event. Over and over I hear clients justify atrocities that have been perpetrated on them.

Susan was a college graduate and the battered wife of a wealthy professional man. They had a magnificent home and two good kids. With pain showing in her half-closed eyes, and sadness etched into her face, she described in vivid detail the horror of the beatings she had endured.

As I gazed at this dear woman who had been treated so cruelly, I wanted to tear her husband limb from limb. Fantasy took over for a second and I could see myself slinging a chair and knocking him, flailing, to the ground, wounded, bleeding—getting what he deserved. I wondered whether there was any way she could have protected herself.

Susan must have sensed my question, for she asked, "What would you have done?" I replied, "Well, I think I would have taken a chair and bashed him with it." She looked at me in horror and said, "But I would have hurt him."

That statement spoke volumes to me. It said Susan could not protect herself. Her self-esteem was too low. Her twisted thought pattern justified her spouse's mistreatment of her. She went on to apologize profusely for not being a perfect wife and mother. She believed the abuse was warranted because she was unable to live up to her husband's expectations. How tragic!

To be angry in an assertive way is healthy. Assertiveness consists of a rational and truthful confrontation. The goal of confronting is to work things out—not to win. An honorable encounter will have these ingredients:

1. *Honest assessment*. State thoughts and feelings about the situation. Tell it the way it is, with gentleness and truth. Stop pretending.
2. *Request input*. Ask for thoughts and feelings.
3. *Listen*. Hear what is being said. Suppress the desire to give constant rebuttal (silently or verbally). Try to understand how the other person feels.

4. *Compromise*. Verbally affirm the other as a person and accept his or her statements. Release your anger.

A few years ago my former spouse, who is remarried, had a massive heart attack. I found myself praying for him with a sincere concern for his well-being. Even though I was hesitant, I wrote him a note. To my great surprise, he answered my communication with kindness and appreciation.

The raging anger is gone. It has been replaced with forgiveness.

## Stage Three: Confrontation

I do not think a person can heal or forgive until he has confronted the person who brought about the pain. When I was a passive person, I swallowed anger and pretended everything was okay. The dishonesty sent the pain underground, but eventually, anger erupted. It came oozing out in snide remarks, criticism, and sarcasm. From that dark pit, forgiveness cannot come.

A lifelong friend hurt me deeply. We had grown up in the same town and possessed a sisterlike bond. Her husband died in an airplane crash several years prior to my divorce. She was left a young widow without children. We became even closer when we were both single again.

Barbara remarried six years after she was widowed. Soon after she met her husband-to-be, our friendship took a slippery slide downhill. By the time of her marriage, our camaraderie, for the most part, was gone. The rejection surprised and hurt me. I had filled a need in her life, as she had in mine. Now that her husband was meeting the need, there was no room in her life for me. This is not to say that a marriage does not change friendships—it should. However, I believe we still need friends of the same sex in order to be balanced and healthy individuals.

In the next few years, Barbara and I saw each other several times and had limited phone conversations. I didn't have the courage to honestly confront how I felt about being rejected. I prayed for forgiveness. It did not come.

One summer day, I called Barbara and asked that we meet for lunch. I had made the decision to be assertive and confront the issues. It was very difficult for me, yet I was honest about my feelings. After we talked, I still did not feel good about the outcome.

A few months later, I wrote Barbara a note similar to this:

> Dear Barbara,
> Just a note to tell you how much our friendship has meant to me over the years.
> You were there for me when I was so hurt from the divorce. You listened, comforted, and loved me.
> When I had the car accident, you stayed with Kathi while I was in the hospital. I never had to ask. You just gave so willingly.
> We've laughed until our sides ached, teased and played. What wonderful memories.
> Thank you for always being there! I do hope there is still a thread of friendship between us and perhaps someday it will be revived.
>
> Love,
> Jeenie

In return, Barbara wrote an endearing letter. We are not back into an intimate friendship and may never be, but I am finally on the road to forgiveness.

Confronting in a gentle, sincere, and truthful manner is strenuous, but it is the road to healing and forgiveness.

# Stage Four: The Acts of Forgiving

Forgiveness is an act of the will. It is a decision. In our minds, we make a *decision*. We *do* something about the decision (*an act*). Then, in time, our feelings catch up with what we originally decided. It is not the other way around. When we base our decisions on feelings, we are in big trouble, for our feelings are up and down, undependable, like a Ferris wheel out of control. We must go first with logic because our minds are more stable than our feelings.

Look at the example of weight loss. If I waited until I felt like losing weight, I would weigh 350 pounds. Instead, I make a logical *decision*, based on my scale. (When it goes around twice, I diet.) I begin the *act* of dieting, such as eating well-balanced meals, counting calories, and exercising. Only when I no longer need to lie on the bed to zip up my jeans, and the scale says I am down ten pounds, do I *feel* like dieting. At this point, my feelings have caught up with my intelligent decision.

There is a similar cycle in forgiving. We make the decision with our *minds*. The *actions* we choose are those that are conducive to forgiveness, ones that propel us toward our goal. In time, we *feel* the healing and forgiveness.

## Self-Forgiveness

Even though I felt I was a good wife, I have scrutinized my role and find there were inconsistencies. Many things were done, said, and thought that were unhealthy for me and the marriage. A great deal of it came from my own low self-esteem and misinformation. I have learned so much since then and could have done things very differently—had I known. I have forgiven myself for being imperfect, human, and naive. Forgiving myself for my part in the failure of the marriage was essential to healing.

With separated/divorced clients, this is an extremely difficult area. Some people tend to constantly go over and over their errors. I hear such things as, ''Sometimes dinner wasn't ready when he came home,'' or ''The trash was usually at the top of the container when I took it out''—as if these insignificant events *caused* the marriage breakup. In truth, it was usually a third-party involvement, not a late meal or a full trash can.

When people continue to berate themselves and are averse to self-forgiveness, the healing can drag on literally forever. Self-pardon is critical.

### Seeking Forgiveness

When I first heard from Jim Smoke (*Growing Through Divorce*) the concept of asking my former mate's forgiveness for my part in the demise of the marriage, I didn't like it. For sure, I was not going to do it. I continued to mull over the dreaded thought for weeks. Finally I came to the conclusion it was valid. I had contributed to the failure. It was necessary to admit it to my former husband, as well as to myself, and declare my need for forgiveness. I chose to do something about my decision.

Picking up the telephone, with palpitating heart and thick tongue, I dialed my former husband. When he answered, I said, ''I've done a lot of thinking about our divorce and realize I had a part in the breakup of the marriage. I'm asking you to forgive me.''

I let go of a heavy load when I chose to ask forgiveness and admit my shortcomings.

# Stage Five: Renewal

For some relationships there is renewal; in others it does not occur. If a renewal is possible and acceptable to both spouses, it will call for intense sessions of honest and sincere dialogue.

John and Bev were a couple in their mid-thirties with three elementary-school-age children. Bev was a homemaker and John commended her as a wife and mother. John worked in a factory on the swing shift.

One of the girls who worked with John was quite loose. Most of the men had been with her sexually (stated John's report). She became pregnant and named John as the father. He swore they had only one sexual encounter.

John and Bev shuffled silently into my office. John was very remorseful. Tears flowed and his whole body was wrenched with the sorrow of his mistake. Weeks before, he had told Bev of the infidelity and expressed his shame. The threat of a paternity suit brought them into counseling.

The court date came. John and Bev glanced nervously at each other as they stepped into the small courtroom. Their anxiety turned to jubilance when the outcome was announced in John's favor.

Both Bev and John worked hard on their marriage in therapy prior to the court appearance and for many months afterward. They were honest about thoughts and feelings. It was important to them to survive this crisis and, in time, have a stable and good marriage. Because of their truthfulness, their willingness to work, and their desire to forgive, renewal was achieved.

Unfortunately, most relationships are not reinstated. In order to have renewal, there must be total honesty. True humility, repentance, and forgiveness are also mandatory. This is extremely difficult. Since many people are reluctant to work out their problems, seldom is there rejuvenation.

If renewal occurs, however, the bond is even stronger.

## Forgive and Forget?

We do not forget! Forgiveness is compulsory, but we will never forget. I can recall, in detail, the ending of my marriage. My memory will never let go of this painful time in my life.

However, the event no longer has significance to me. Because I am healed and have forgiven, it no longer impacts my life.

I was with my daughter, Kathi, in the labor room of a large metropolitan hospital. After many hours of labor, her doctor decided to take the baby by cesarean section, so I left to wait in another area.

As I rounded the corner, a man down the hall said, "Hi." Squinting at him, I thought, *Who is he? Why is he saying hi?* I sneaked another glance.

My heart jumped. It was my former husband. Unable to respond appropriately, I tensely returned a rather lame greeting.

Minutes later, with excitement and gratitude, we were peering in the window of the nursery at the tiny, pink baby boy. As my former husband, his wife, and I were chatting, thoughts were tumbling through my mind. *I can't believe I ever knew this man. It's even more astounding that I was married to him and loved him deeply. It seems unreal—like a dream—foggy.*

Even though I recall nearly all the facts, the significance of them is gone. The incidents no longer affect my life.

## Don't Rush Forgiveness

Many of you are recently out of a marriage, and the thought of forgiveness is abhorrent. These feelings are quite normal. Forgiveness takes *time*. It is unwise to try to forgive too early because you have not been in the stages of healing long enough. Someone who has been separated a few weeks, six months, or even a year is not a candidate for dealing heavily with forgiveness.

So, give yourself permission to heal.

In time, I wish you freedom, wholeness, and healing through the channel of forgiveness.

# Insight for Growth

1. Imagine we are in our counseling room. Face your former spouse and say, "I am willing to forgive you."

2. Tell me what you are feeling.

3. Turn to your former mate again and say, "Will you forgive me for the part I had in the failure of our marriage?"

4. Again, tell me what you feel.

5. What things are preventing you from beginning the forgiveness process?

# 7

# SINGLE PARENTING
## (The Job Nobody Wants)

Tears splashed on the arm of the sofa as my patient slumped into the cushions. "I just can't stand this anymore. As if the divorce wasn't bad enough—now I've got out-of-control kids. They blame me for this whole mess. When my teens get mad, I keep hearing, 'Hey, I'm gonna split and live with Dad. This place is a drag. Get off my back, will you? I'm outta here.' As a mom, it's more than I can handle," she sobbed.

Is it ever!

It is difficult to raise a family with both parents; alone, it can be horrendous.

Looking into the sad brown eyes of another young mother, I saw tears beginning to well. Breathlessly she said, "I got my little ones ready for their daddy. They were so excited, they sat on the porch for an hour waiting. Then, two hours. He never came. What could I tell them? Their little hearts were broken and they couldn't understand why Daddy didn't come. I held them in my arms and rocked them until the tears stopped and sleep quieted their pain. I could have killed him."

"My little girl is going to be a teenager," a father said. Catching my eye, he immediately dropped his head and in a lower, softer voice continued, "I don't know how to talk to her about those female things. She really needs her mom. But my wife's off with her boyfriend and couldn't care less what happens to these kids. Maybe she doesn't want me, but how could she leave her own flesh and blood? Sometimes I feel so helpless."

"Those kids mean the world to me," another man whispered. "They're my whole life." Awkwardly he brushed away the tears. "My ex just won't let me see them. If I call, she hangs up. I send them cards and gifts, but I get no response. They probably never get them. It's all so unfair."

Pain for the parents. Pain for the kids. The emotional upheaval makes single parenting even more demanding and difficult.

Fortunately, there are ways to make parenting more productive and less of an ordeal. The end result will be more positive, and a good relationship can unfold during the journey. As parents, we don't have to continue to muddle through. There is hope.

## Listen to Your Kids

"My parents *never* listen!"

If I had a dollar for every time I've heard that statement, I would be sunning on Waikiki Beach instead of sitting at this computer! Kids really open up when we are willing to shut up and let them express their inner feelings.

Vividly I remember a time I did not listen to my child. The steam was rising from the stove top while the microwave incessantly screamed its rhythmic message, trying to be heard above the barking dog announcing the doorbell. My junior high daughter was talking and talking and talking. I was feigning interest.

Wanting my daughter to think I was an interested, concerned parent, I interjected a question. (Actually, I was quite proud of myself for simulating concern so convincingly.)

She exploded, "I just *told* you that. You weren't listening, were you? I knew it. You *never* listen to me."

My mind formed a perfect answer: *Oh, but I was listening to you, my dear.* Instead, I decided to be honest. "Kathi, I'm really sorry. I was not listening, but I want to. If you'll run through it again, I promise to listen this time." Grudgingly she complied.

Bedtime brought the incident back to mind and I pondered, *How can I really listen to my daughter?* A thought came to me: *Sit on the floor with her.*

Sitting on the floor has become a splendid way for me to be intently involved. Several things happen on the floor: first, there's not much else to do while I'm down there; second, it is easy to make eye contact; third, touching can more naturally take place.

Floors are wonderful places to be close, share emotions, have fun, shed tears, touch, wrestle, connect—all the things that make for real and vulnerable communication. The walls come down. Even though I'm in my overstuffed chair during a therapy session, in my mind I'm sitting on the floor with my client.

Dialing the phone, my friend's "Hi" was what I wanted to hear. "I'm feeling awful," I responded. "I'm hurt and angry and I just need you to listen to me. I don't want any advice—just a listening ear."

"You got it," she replied. The she proceeded to give me what I desired: a nonjudgmental and uninterrupted period of time.

By saying exactly what I was feeling, I was able to work through the issues. Solutions began to come to me as I talked.

Often we can figure out the answers if we have the opportunity to talk it through with someone who is willing to listen.

Kids need that, too.

As parents, we are not only emotionally involved but we also have a great responsibility as to how our children turn out. It's scary. Too often we jump on our soapbox and preach a little— sometimes a lot. It would be better for both parent and child if we earned the right to be heard by listening first.

## Fact-Versus-Feeling Message

Windows rattled as the teen stormed into the kitchen, slamming doors. With a wild expression and blazing eyes, she screamed, "I hate that teacher! I got an *F* in math."

"You got *what* in math, young lady?" her mother screamed. "Well, no wonder. If I've asked you once, I've asked you a million times if you have any homework. But no. It's always no. No homework, nothing to do. You're always doing okay. 'Don't sweat it, Mom,' I keep hearing. Now you've gone and gotten an *F*. Unbelievable. You're just too much."

This mom responded to the *factual* message, which is what most of us tend to do.

Let's change Mom's response. This time she will respond to the *feeling* message first:

"I hate that teacher! I got an *F* in math," Debbie screamed.

"Deb, it sounds as if you had a horrible day at school," Mom responded. "Want to tell me what happened?"

"You just wouldn't believe it, Mom." Tears began to well as the teen continued. "Miss Burnett called me up to the board to work out a math problem. I was so nervous, I couldn't remember how to do it. My mind went blank. She kept hinting at things, but I didn't know what she was talking about. I felt hot all over.

" 'Well, go sit down,' Miss Burnett told me. 'It's obvious you're not willing to try. You've just earned another *F*, and at this rate you can count on failing the whole class.'

"Mom, I've never been so humiliated in my whole life. I was really trying, but I just couldn't think. Everyone was laughing and I felt like a fool. It was all I could do to keep from running out the door," Deb continued. "I never want to go back to that school. I just can't face everybody."

"Oh, sweetie," Mom responded. "It must have been terrible. I feel for you, and I'm so very sorry it happened. Math hasn't always been your easiest subject, but I know how hard you work trying to understand it. I'll call the school and see if we can get some tutoring to help you understand. I also want to talk to Miss Burnett."

When we respond to the *facts* first, we cut off communication. Because Deb got a lecture from Mom, there was no way in the world she would tell her about the embarrassment and terrible day. Deb would think, *Mom never listens to me—she doesn't care.* It wouldn't be true, but that's how her mom would come across.

All of us have a need to have our *feeling* messages heard. When we feel understood, we are more capable of dealing with the facts.

Most of the time, the feeling message comes *first*. The factual news tags along.

Picture an eight-year-old boy in a torn baseball uniform, covered with mud. Tears begin to splash down his face and with his grubby little hand, mixing moisture with dirt, he smears away the tears. Sobbing, he says, "I'm not going back to baseball *ever*. I never wanted to play in the first place, and I lost my glove."

*Fact Response*: "Your glove? You lost your glove?" yelled

Mom. "How can you be so careless? Grandpa bought that for you. You don't care about anything, do you? Boy, will he be mad when he finds out. He'll never get you anything again and I can't blame him a bit."

Stalking out of the kitchen, Mom turned around and hollered, "I see you also tore your uniform. You know, I scrimped and saved to buy you that outfit and now it's ruined. It'll be a long time before you get anything again."

*Feeling Response*: "Oh, Bobby, it looks as if something awful happened to you. Come here, dear, and tell me about it."

"Well, I got up to bat and struck out," Bobby blurted. "We had all these guys on base and everybody was yelling for me to hit a homer. I was shaking, the bat was slipping, and I just couldn't hit the ball. I made us lose the game. All the guys were telling me I was the worst one on the team. I cried all the way home and fell over a rock because I couldn't see, and I lost the glove Grandpa got me."

Mom held him close and softly said, "Bobby, I'm so very sorry. I know it really hurts. You've practiced hard at baseball and Dad thinks you've really improved. We're really proud of you, son."

Kissing Bobby lightly on the forehead, Mom continued, "Now, why don't you take a nice, warm shower. I've got one of your favorite dinners almost ready. Then after we eat, we'll go out looking for your mitt."

When we jump the gun and deal with the factual information, we never find out how the person really feels. When this happens, it produces an emotional tear. If it becomes a pattern, the child will close off emotionally so he or she won't be hurt anymore. This can do great relational harm that may carry into adulthood. I counsel so many emotionally handicapped people who were damaged as children.

When we respond to the feeling message first, it is an act of love and will create bonding. It will also set the emotional stage for dealing with the facts at a more appropriate time.

## Punishment or Discipline?

There is a big difference between punishment and discipline. Punishment is a form of getting back at "that sucker." "Get in your room and stay there until I say to come out!" we bellow. Actually, we are planning to shove food and water under the door until he turns eighteen!

Discipline demands creativity and consistency. First, you have to calm down. When you react in anger, the result is almost always punishment. Second, ask yourself, "What can I do that will produce lasting change?"

"Man, am I ever sick of that teacher! He's always on my case. The worst part is I have him for two classes a day," the teen exploded.

"Tell me what happened, Chris," I suggested.

"Well, it's no big deal. I got a drink and a little bit of water sort of went out of my mouth," he retorted.

On the referral form, the teacher stated, "I'm sick of this kid. We've had parent conferences, but nothing has helped. He took a mouthful of water and spit it. I want his hide."

"Sounds like Mr. Martinez is really angry with you. He probably gave you a lecture and sent you in here to get another one from me, plus some detention," I said.

Hanging his head, he mumbled, "Uh-huh."

"Chris, I think it's time Mr. Martinez, your parents, and I got off your back," I announced.

He lifted his head. His eyes widened.

"I'll make a deal with you," I continued. "I'll inform Mr. Martinez that the next time you do something wrong in class, he quietly hands you a referral that says 'counselor'—no lectures. You come in here and I'll not even ask what you did. Instead, I'll give you two hours of detention. No speeches. Now, since you have him for both math and science, you could get as much as four hours of detention every day. The choice is yours, Chris.

"The next time you get a drink and decide to spit, I suggest you fill your mouth until it nearly bursts, let that water go, and get everyone in the room in one fell swoop," I summed up. "Make it count, because you'll have two hours of detention. Of course, you can also think about the detention while water is leaking out of your mouth and decide to swallow it. Whatever you choose is okay with me."

Chris never came back. A few years after graduation, he peeked in my office door, came bounding in, and gave me a hug. He was a fine young man whose life was going well because he was making good choices. This was exactly what I was hoping for when I meted out the disciplinary measure years before.

It is much easier to be a good disciplinarian with other people's teens. With our own, we are bombarded day in and day out, and we are emotionally involved. But we can learn to discipline rather than punish. The results are worth the struggle.

## Setting Limits

All of us need limits, especially kids. In giving parameters, we tell the child precisely what we expect and exactly what will happen if it does not occur. Parent and child can sign a written agreement.

Parent:   "Your curfew is eleven o'clock Friday night. If there is a problem, I expect to be called before eleven. If you are late and haven't called, you will not be allowed to go out next Friday and Saturday evenings."

Surprise, surprise! The teen comes in at half-past eleven and "forgot" to telephone.

Parent:   "Kristy, tell me what happened."
Kristy:   "Well, we were just kickin' back and I forgot."
Parent:   "We had a deal, Kristy. You will not be able to go out next Friday and Saturday nights."
Kristy:   "That's not fair! How can you do this to me? I bought my ticket for the amusement park already—with my own money."
Parent:   "*Regardless*, you did not live up to our contract."
Kristy:   "How stupid! You make me sick. I earned this money and I'm going."
Parent:   "Kristy, you are not going. You did not live up to our contract."
Kristy:   "You're so mean!"
Parent:   "*Regardless*, you did not live up to our contract."

The parent outlined the limits as well as the consequences at the beginning. This saves making up answers later. Also, the parent kept to the subject by using "regardless" and stating a phrase over and over (Broken Record). The teen would soon realize her parent was not going to argue.

Walking into ten-year-old Jimmy's room was like entering a disaster area. One could hardly see the floor, let alone the bed. The place smelled. Mom was at her wits' end. No amount of screaming worked. *So,* she thought, *maybe I should try something different.*

| | |
|---|---|
| Mom: | "Jimmy, could I see you a minute?" |
| Jimmy: | "Yeah, Mom, what do you want?" |
| Mom: | "I want everything picked up off your bed and the floor, then put away in either your closet or drawers. This needs to be done by tomorrow evening at seven o'clock. If it is not, I'll stick it all in a trash bag and you'll have to buy each piece back for a dime. Do you understand what I want, Jimmy?" |
| Jimmy: | "Sure." |
| Mom: | "Tell me what I've asked you to do." |
| Jimmy: | "Pick up my stuff." |
| Mom: | "From where?" |
| Jimmy: | "The bed and floor." |
| Mom: | "And?" |
| Jimmy: | "Put in my closet or drawers." |
| Mom: | "When?" |
| Jimmy: | "Tomorrow, seven o'clock. Will you leave me alone?" |
| Mom: | "One more thing. If you don't, what happens?" |
| Jimmy: | "I have to give you a dime for each piece." |
| Mom: | "Okay, that's our deal. Agreed?" |
| Jimmy: | "Yeah, yeah." |

The next day, at 7:01 P.M., Mom goes into Jimmy's room. No change.

| Mom: | "Jimmy, I want to see you, please." |
| Jimmy: | "Yeah, Mom, what?" |
| Mom: | "Yesterday, I told you that your room had to have everything off the floor and bed and in your closet or dresser by seven o'clock this evening. I see it's not done, so I will bag it up and you can buy it back for ten cents each." |
| Jimmy: | "Hey, no. I was busy. Don't do that." |
| Mom: | "You did not live up to our agreement, Jimmy." |
| Jimmy: | "Mom, I promise I'll pick it up." |
| Mom: | "Sorry, son, it's too late." |
| Jimmy: | "That's not fair. How would you like it if I did that to all your stuff, huh?" |
| Mom: | "*Regardless*, you did not live up to our agreement." |

When we articulate *precisely* what we want and by what time, it is easier to hold the line. We can mete out the previously stated discipline without getting out of control or emotional. The yelling stops. We step out of the parent/child trap and make children accountable to us, *regardless* of what excuses they use.

## Rescuing

In the setting of limits, it is imperative that we allow children to take the consequences of their actions. Don't rescue!
Kids believe:

1. Everything will turn out okay.
2. Someone will always get me out of a mess.
3. Nothing will really happen to me.

These thoughts float through their minds because they are true. They are true because adults have covered for children for years. Young people are often not required to deal with the repercussions of their actions.

Rescuing is one of the worst disservices we can do to our kids. Eventually it leads to trauma and pain.

At graduation time, I've nicknamed my high school office "The Wailing Wall." After four years of telling teens (and their parents), "You're behind in credits . . . these are the classes you must take in summer school . . . here's a referral card for adult school to make up the required class you failed. . . . You've failed three more classes . . . before long, it's going to be too late," they are shocked to learn graduation is not a possibility. Pulling out warning letter after warning letter from the files does not convince the parents.

"Grandma is flying in from Omaha," they sob. "You just can't do this to us. Besides, we spent all this money on graduation pictures. Something has to be done."

When the tears don't work, they sometimes go up the educational hierarchy only to hear, "We're sorry, but there's nothing we can do. It's too late."

It is amazing how many of these parents have never responded to my letters or calls over the years. The first time I see some of them is when they rush into my office in answer to the "Non-Grad" letter.

Then, there's the student. . . .

"Mrs. Gordon, I know I can do it. I'm ready now to pop out these four classes. I mean business this time. There are two weeks left and I'll work at adult school every night until they close. I just have to graduate. Nothing can stop me," he promises. Unfortunately, he doesn't have enough time to finish even one class, let alone four.

He does not meet the graduation deadline.

During finals, I call him into my office and gently say, "Jeff, I know you're disappointed about graduation. It must really hurt to realize you won't be involved in the ceremonies. Even though you will not be graduating, you are *not* a failure. I believe in you and know you can still get your diploma. You can turn this around. Plan to finish your course work by the end of August, and I will hold your diploma. Count on me to be here to hand it to you with pride."

Some teens are devastated because they have passed a point of no return and have not become familiar with facing the painful consequences of their choices. Parents have rescued; so have teachers and counselors. Kids haven't had to face the hard realities of life. They are so unprepared. They have been done a great injustice.

Making kids responsible for their actions is easier said than done. Only if children are allowed to experience logical consequences when they are young can they begin to learn the value of making good decisions by thinking ahead about possible results. By the time they reach adulthood, they are much better equipped to choose responsibly and take the consequences of their selections.

My advice is to quit covering for them, getting them off the hook, lying for them, or excusing their actions. Instead, allow them to be impacted by their decisions. It is difficult for us to sit back and see them experience pain, but in the long run, it is the more loving response.

# Concentrate on the "Biggies"

As parents, too often we come apart over trivial actions and fads. We yell so much that by the time the big stuff comes along, our energy is gone, we're hoarse, and the kids have stopped listening.

During the seventies era of long-haired teen boys, a mother and father constantly complained to their son, "You look awful. Get a haircut. We're ashamed to be seen with you. It's disgusting."

It always surprised me, because his hair was shiny, clean, and always well brushed. I never thought the length was that important.

One day after school, mother and son were shopping in the supermarket. Walking up to the checkout stand, Tim flipped his head backward to get the hair out of his eyes. Since his hair fell in his eyes a lot, this was a rather frequent motion.

Mom was angry. "Do you know how stupid you look, always flipping your head back that way? This is how it looks." She then then gave a vibrant flip of the head and turned in horror to watch her wig sliding across the tiled floor. At home, she had hurriedly put on the wig because her hair was dirty. Now the limp, greasy strands were stuck to the contours of her skull. Lamely, she picked up the wig and slapped it back on. Tim smiled.

Now, nearly fifteen years later, his hair is still long and he is an exemplary young man, a published musician in the Christian market.

It is so easy to get upset over the trivial. Yet, how difficult (and wise) it is to put our energies into relationships. People endure. Fads fade.

# Separate the Act From the Person

I have seen hundreds of teens who curse out their parents, run away from home, are alcoholic, take drugs, get pregnant, have abortions, are sexually promiscuous, cut school, lie, go to jail, and commit murder. Yet I've had deep, loving bonds with some of these kids, regardless of what they have done.

All of us do wrong things, sometimes because we are ignorant, other times because we are just plain mad. Just because we do wrong things does not make us bad people. The acts are separate from who we really are.

I have learned to look beyond the behavior and into the tender soul of the person. That's not to say I excuse the wrong deed, but I want to get to the root of it. When we are willing to connect at the feeling level, changes can occur.

Jason sauntered into my office, slumped in the chair, and looked about as alert as a turnip. *Oh, boy, one of those*, I thought. Then, looking at him carefully, I questioned, *Why would a young man be so uninterested in life? He's certainly got a lot going for him.*

Jason had come into his senior year of high school so far behind in credits that graduation was virtually impossible. Drinking and drugs filled his weekends. To him, life was a drag and he couldn't care less.

*Someone has to care about this kid*, I thought. *I wonder if I could ever get through to him.*

"Jason," I queried, "if there were no holds barred, what would you like to be in life?"

"Huh?" he responded.

"Looking at you, I see a really fine young man—a person who has so much potential. You are intelligent, good looking, and I'll bet a great worker when you make up your mind. Whatever has possessed you to get your life in such a mess is beyond me. What a waste, Jason. You know, I really believe in you. You have the ability and intelligence to be whatever you want. I challenge you, Jason, to turn this graduation status around. The work is up to you, but I'm here to give you ideas and encouragement. You can count on me."

Eyes brightening, he said, "You think I really could graduate?"

"With a lot of hard work, I *know* you can," I answered. "Okay, here's the plan. . . ."

Jason's smile was as brilliant as the June moon on graduation evening. He screamed, threw his hat, and grabbed me in a bear hug. "I made it! I really did it!" he exulted.

Over the next few years, Jason often stopped by to chat and keep me up on his life. "Hey, favorite counselor," he bellowed on one occasion as he popped into my office. "I've got a crazy idea and I want your input. I'm thinking of changing colleges again. The first two years I stayed at the community college, now I'm finishing my junior year at Cal State University, but I've always wanted to be a U.C.L.A. graduate. Does that sound dumb? Should I try transferring for my senior year?"

"Go for it, Jason. Put in for the transfer. All they can do is say no. It's always worth it to follow your dream," I replied.

During his senior year at U.C.L.A., Jason worked part-time in the engineering department of the famous Jet Propulsion Laboratory and was offered a permanent position upon graduation.

"Hey, look what I have for you," he beamed one lazy afternoon. He handed me a poster of the rocket on which he had worked. With tear-filled eyes, he softly said, "You're the only person who has ever believed in me. Had it not been for you, I wouldn't have graduated from high school, let alone from college. You gave me encouragement, a listening ear, and an incentive to achieve.''

It is human to look beyond the potential and see only how a kid has messed up his life. But when we can separate the actions from the person, miracles seem to happen, for we all tend to live up to the expectations of the people we admire.

I have seen dramatic changes in teens who were runaways, on drugs, sexually promiscuous, truants, inmates, and just plain average because I was willing to see them as people who desperately needed love and someone to accept them as they were.

## Green Apples

We had a stately, sprawling apple tree in our backyard when I was four years old. My idea of a great time was to laboriously climb into the branches, choose a sturdy limb, straddle it, and eat apples to my heart's content. On one occasion, I was unwilling to wait until the apples turned red. They looked too inviting, so I ate my fill—of little green ones. After a terrible tummyache, I learned that apples need to ripen.

Kids are rather like apples. It takes a long time for them to mature. So often, we want to "pick them" in June, but they won't be ready until fall.

Fall does come.

## It's Worth It

It is tremendously hard to go it alone. Fatigue is a constant companion, and we are often worn down by struggle and worry. Nevertheless, I have witnessed hundreds of youths from single-parent families grow into responsible citizens. As adults, they often commend their parents with great pride and acclaim because they know the burden of single parenting. Through the hard times, they learn invaluable lessons that eventually will enable them to become healthy mates and parents. They have seen struggle as well as survival firsthand.

Someday, it will be worth it.

# Insight for Growth

Mark the following statements using: Low (Almost Never),
Middle (Sometimes), or High (Almost Always).

Low scores suggest change is indicated.
Middle scores are okay but may need a little work.
High scores indicate good parenting skills.

1. It is important for me to *really* listen to my child. I try to fully
   concentrate on what he or she is saying without giving a lot of
   advice.

2. Usually I respond to the feeling message first and deal with
   the facts later.

3. Most of the time I discipline rather than punish my offspring.

4. I refuse to argue with my kid. I state what I want and stick to
   the subject (i.e., *"Regardless . . ."*).

5. I stay clear of rescuing. I allow my child to experience the
   logical consequences of his or her actions.

6. Usually I let the minor things go and save my energy for the "biggies."

7. Most of the time I separate the act from the person. I try to encourage my offspring and set reasonable standards.

Score yourself and notice the pattern that emerges. It will help you pinpoint areas of strength as well as weakness. Set a goal to work on one weak area at a time. Good luck!

# 8

# RELAX? YOU'VE GOT TO BE KIDDING!

Stress is such a common phenomenon in our lives that it is unlikely a day can pass without someone saying, "I'm stressed out."

Being separated/divorced brings additional stress. There are toilets to be fixed, dishes to be washed, groceries to buy, lawns waiting to be mowed, bills piled up, dirty laundry stacked, an undependable, broken-down car, kids needing both a mom and dad—and *one* person to do it all. Nothing is shared. There is no spouse to take some of the load.

When people comment on "all the free time you have because you're single," I get mad! If I begin to list the things I am required to do, they get quiet—fast.

A nineteen-year-old aspiring medical student had one of those "inquiring minds that want to know." However, when he began questioning his professor at the German University of Prague, he was met with a stern lecture. As Hans Selye postulated his theory about stress, the older and wiser prof looked him squarely in the eye and stated, "Such theorizing is best left to more experienced scientists."

So young Hans kept quiet, but his mind continued to explore. He completed his doctorate in organic chemistry and in 1936 published an article on generalized stress reaction in a British scientific journal. Again he was met with controversy and ridicule from his colleagues because of his absurd ideas.

Selye had coined the word *stress* to portray how the body responds to emotional stimuli (i.e., fear, anger, and so on). Undaunted, he continued research on "stressors" and finally was recognized in 1976 as an honored scientist.

Dr. Selye believed there is good stress (eustress) and bad stress.

Eustress propels us into action. It is a motivator to get us going. We feel good about ourselves and what we accomplish. Being launched into action is not the same as being *controlled* by stress. We move forward but are not driven.

Negative stress produces *distress*. It affects us emotionally and physically in a conceivably damaging way. It can deter us from reaching our potential.

In an interview published in *Psychology Today* (March 1979), Selye discussed two types of people: the "racehorses," who thrive on stress and are happy with a vigorous, fast-paced lifestyle, and the "turtles," who need peace, quiet, and a generally tranquil environment. However, he believed we all need to look for signs that indicate we are stressed and practice alleviation of these stressors.

Nowadays, just about everyone has jumped on the bandwagon. Even the "common folk" realize our bodies do respond to our emotions.

# Stressors

Our *surroundings* produce stress. For instance, smog and freeways—need I say more? There are also sirens wailing, kids screaming, TVs blaring, radios blasting, horns honking, and dogs barking. We are bombarded with this type of stressor, and our bodies react to it.

*Guilt* is a culprit. Actually, there are two kinds of guilt: real and false. Suppose I took a sawed-off shotgun and blasted someone. If I didn't feel intense guilt, something would be drastically wrong. Real guilt can spur us to action, to turn our lives around, to make recompense.

Then there is false guilt. Whenever someone uses a lot of "shoulds" and "oughts," he or she is probably suffering from false guilt. Always trying to please others, making things okay for everybody else, feeling responsible for everything and everyone can be symptoms of false guilt, which is most likely caused by a low self-image.

*Internal stressors* come from our negative thoughts, feelings, and expectations. We feed ourselves with a daily diet of pessimistic self-talk. You think, *it's no wonder I'm going through a divorce. What ever made me think I have what it takes to hold on to a husband/wife?*

*Corporations* promote stress. They want to keep us busy and do it with rules, deadlines, and inordinately high expectations. Some companies even deliberately create stress in order to do more business, develop a name for themselves, and make big bucks. We can be caught right in the middle of it.

Then there are *relational stressors* from a boss, kids, wife, husband, parents, extended family, friends, neighbors, and even a yipping dog. We are constantly called on to relate, even when we're tired, hungry, irritable, and just plain don't care.

An *unforgiving spirit* that houses hatred, resentment, and bitterness brings on stress like gang busters. Chapter 6 is devoted to
this important issue.

*Procrastination* was my undoing. This seemingly small obsta-
cle is a great stressor. I have spent hours feeling guilty about what
I "should" accomplish, but a good TV program or short nap
usually ended my stress—until the next day, or until I was up
against a deadline, or when I had missed it and found myself in
deep trouble.

Actually, almost everything in life can be stress-producing if
we allow it.

## Symptoms of Stress

Stress affects us physically, emotionally, and behaviorally.
Many physicians are now suggesting that perhaps 85 percent of
all diseases are stress-related. That's scary! Conversely, it is
hopeful. It says to me that we have great power and control over
our bodies. We have choices.

*Physical* symptoms include fatigue, aches and pains, gas-
trointestinal problems, asthma, cardiovascular difficulties, stomach distress, migraines, rapid heartbeat, colitis, shortness of
breath, dizziness, and heartburn.

A few of the *emotional* responses are depression, anger, anxiety, nightmares, and sleep disturbances.

*Behaviorally*, we can experience such things as daydreaming,
indecisiveness, alcohol and drug abuse, fidgeting, and eating
disorders.

"Sounds like a pretty bleak picture," you say. Maybe you

have checked off a bunch of the symptoms and now are really feeling stressed.

The good news is that there is hope!

## Adrenaline and Stress

After reading numerous books and articles on stress, I came across a wonderful book, *The Hidden Link Between Adrenalin & Stress* by Dr. Archibald D. Hart. It had great impact on my stress-reduction journey.

Adrenaline is advantageous to us for two purposes: to flee or to fight. Imagine a man rushing into the room where you are sitting with ten other people. As you look more closely, you realize he has a gun. Your eyes immediately enlarge, your heart pounds, palms sweat, and adrenaline rushes to your brain.

*This guy's a little dude,* you think. *There are four of us behind him and we can give him a shove, knock the gun from his hand, and get him to the floor. We can take him—no problem.* At that moment, your physical strength becomes superhuman and you go into action to conquer.

Or maybe you decide, *I have to get out of here, but the gunman is blocking the door.* Your eyes search for a window. *It's pretty high,* you think, *but it's only a short drop outside. I'm going for it.* With the aim of a speeding bullet, you jump on the wall, kick in the window, smash through, and leap to the pavement. You can hardly remember the last time you climbed out a window let alone one halfway up a wall, closed and locked. But high energy coursed through your veins and you escaped.

The local newspaper carried a story about a father who lifted an automobile off his small son, saving his life. At the moment

of desperate need, adrenaline exploded into his brain and the dad
had extraordinary strength to perform a superhuman feat.

According to Dr. Hart, we encounter a problem when we
become addicted to adrenaline for ordinary, daily living. He
states:

> It is actually possible for us to become addicted to our own
> adrenalin! We can get hooked on the pleasurable "high"
> that comes from the workings of the body's defense system.
> This adrenalin creates a surge of energy to help the body
> respond to the stressful challenge. And this surge of activity
> often feels good! Pain is suppressed and we feel excited and
> powerful. We become hooked on the "adrenalin high" to
> the point that we crave it over and over. We learn to
> "psych" ourselves up to a high level of adrenalin arousal
> with certain actions and attitudes just to feel good.

He further explains that when the rush of adrenaline goes to the
brain, heart, and lungs, it leaves the extremities. They then become cold. One simple test is to touch your fingers to your face.
If your fingers are colder than your face, your adrenaline is up.
And, says Hart, "the greater the difference in temperature between hands and face, the greater the stress reaction."

I began working consistently on stress reduction by reading
everything I could get my hands on, then practicing the concepts.
When my adrenaline is up and I feel stressed, I walk into my
office, close the door, sit in a chair, close my eyes, place my
forearms on the arms of the chair, dangle my fingers, and in
about one minute, I can almost feel the stress dripping out through
my fingers onto the floor. My hands become warm and my whole
body feels rested. I have practiced this at home, in bathrooms, on
benches, at airports, or wherever the need arises.

When I'm relaxed, my energy level is up, I feel calm, and I become very productive.

In looking through Hart's research again for this segment, I retook the stress tests. The first ones were taken three years ago. In all of them, my score is lower. My stress is even more in control.

## Stresslessness

It was Friday, August 6. The day before, my church tour group had visited the magnificent Neuschwanstein Castle in Germany. We were awestruck at its architectural beauty, flowering gardens, and ornate rooms. History came alive as we meandered through the chambers. Disney was enamored with it, too, and replicated it with his "Sleeping Beauty Castle."

That evening we were delighted by the sights and sounds of Munich. We enjoyed the hearty food, ogled the high-fashion models and clothes, shopped for Hummels and handcrafted wooden Christmas ornaments, and walked the streets trying to capture every observation to store in our memories forever.

As our bus rolled into Dachau the next morning, all frivolity was gone. We numbly stared at the fences topped with rolled barbed wire.

Dachau was the first Nazi concentration camp. It was constructed in 1933 and became the model for thirty-six more during World War II. At the information center, we viewed grotesque pictures that began at the floor and ended at the ceiling—one giant photo of emaciated corpses.

The camp was built to house five thousand prisoners, yet it never held fewer than twelve thousand. Going through the dormitories, we could envision bodies cramped into compartments and smell the stench of the urine and vomit of human beings who were dying of dysentery and typhus. In those terrifying, hopeless years, breakfast consisted of bread and coffee. Lunch was thin soup. Dinner entertainment was provided by the parading of naked, terminally ill prisoners. The evening was topped off with beatings.

The once filthy gas chambers had been cleaned and scrubbed, but we could still picture the muck and slime through which the withered dead were transported to their final resting place: the ovens.

Multiplied thousands were tortured, killed, and died of unnatural causes before Liberation Day, March 1, 1945.

Never will the scenes leave my memory.

It is said that stress did not exist in the Nazi camps for four reasons:

*First,* emotions were freely expressed among the prisoners. They talked about their anger, fear, sadness, and hatred.

*Second,* there was no conflict of duty or conscience. No one was trying to excel or get ahead. There was no corporate ladder to climb.

*Third,* there were no face-saving activities. They huddled together, saw each other nude, and used nonprivate toilet facilities. They were down to the bare existence of life, where no one needed or cared to impress anyone else.

*Fourth,* no decisions had to be made. They robotlike followed directions. Whatever they needed to do to survive, they did.

It is interesting that, with our plush and pleasant life-style, we elicit stress because we tend to do the opposite. We keep feelings inside, have internal struggle over duty and conscience, try to look good to everyone, and stew over decisions.

# Healthy Coping Mechanisms

We can drastically reduce stress by being aware of its existence, setting goals, and making good mental health choices.

It is vital to become aware of when our stress level is too high and our adrenaline is up. We have a responsibility to learn how stress can be reduced and put the knowledge into practice. For instance, learn a variety of relaxation methods, adhere to a schedule of regular exercise, be sure to get adequate rest, and choose healthy foods. The more we learn about our bodies, the better we are equipped to cut the stress level to a minimum.

I had a choice when my stress level topped out. I could have ignored it, and only God knows what might have happened to me physically, emotionally, and spiritually. I could have read all those wonderful articles and books, taken tests about stress, yet never put the concepts into practice.

Setting goals is the next step. "Just how much stress am I willing to live with?" I asked myself. I made my determination by looking at the results of the various tests. In the areas where I was high, I made a written plan for what I would do to reduce it. Usually I worked on one or two things at a time. I posted the list on the bathroom mirror so I could read it daily. Those goals became part of me, and many times I was working toward them even when I was not conscious of it. It is not enough to say, "Well, I'd sure like to get rid of a lot of this stress," then do nothing about it. For sure, nothing will happen.

Changing isn't easy. It is deliberate, slow, and can be discouraging. But it finally works.

When I'm stressed out, I think this phrase over and over: *Enough is enough!* By the time I'm saying it aloud, I listen to myself and realize I've got to do something about it. Generally,

I look at my schedule for the next five to seven days and begin cutting everything I can. Unless I'm obligated and will let others down, I cancel out. Just the act reduces stress and in about two days, I'm fine. Because I've been practicing daily (and hourly) stress reduction for several years, I sense when I'm on the edge. I know one more job or event will put me over. Usually, I say no at this point. The times I don't listen, however, and do just *one* more thing, stress knocks me off my feet. I lie there in a heap thinking, *I should have listened.*

Another good choice is to let off steam to a trusted friend or two. When things become overwhelming, talk about it. It is especially helpful when you are in a stressful circumstance over which you have little control. Stress is reduced and life is more bearable.

Also, don't sweat the small stuff. So often, we come unglued over minor incidents—things that have no lasting impact or value.

"I could kill that kid!" a mother thundered as she flew into my office. "Can you believe this? She's only twelve and she up and shaved her legs without asking. I'm her mom and I say what she can do and what she can't." I allowed her rampage to continue. Finally, with a heave of her chest, she tipped her head, squinted, and said, "You don't think it's all that big a deal, do you?"

"Well," I responded, "I think you should save all this emotion for the big stuff—like when your *son* shaves his legs!"

## Laughter, the Great Medicine

Laughter is one of life's greatest stress reducers. Television sitcoms are my favorite. I've watched them all at one time or another. Most are ridiculous, but so am I, so I really get into them and scream with laughter. After a show or two, I feel great.

Parties are my favorite pastime. I usually go to one a week. Sometimes the party is dull, so I liven it up! There are always a few people who are willing to let go and laugh and, before long, most of the group has joined in. Laughter is euphoric. We are left feeling lighthearted, carefree, and stressless.

Taking the advertisement out of my mailbox, I almost threw it into the trash. (I open all my mail over the trash can.) "Not *another* conference," I sighed. Turning the bright red brochure over, I noticed the title: "The Power of Laughter and Play." *Hmmm, sounds better all the time,* I thought. Before long, I became engrossed in the seminar descriptions. Dialing my therapist friend I said, "Hey, there's a conference in March that looks like loads of fun. Want to go?"

The famed comedians Steve Allen and Sid Caesar, with their M.D. sons, started off the evening. Father and son Allen bantered back and forth until we could hardly endure any more laughter. Fifteen hundred professionals wiped tears, held our stomachs, and nearly begged them to stop.

In the following days, not only did we laugh our way through the workshops but we also learned the positive ways our bodies and emotions respond to laughter.

The previous year's keynote speaker, Norman Cousins (on videotape), told of his recovery from a life-threatening malady by using several unorthodox measures. Dr. Cousins roared with laughter by watching old movies of the Marx Brothers and other comics. He found that fifteen minutes of hearty laughter gave him two pain-free hours. He believed laughter releases endorphins (nature's painkillers) into the system.

Dr. Annette Goodheart stated in her workshop that laughter exercises the respiratory system, can work as a painkiller, may reduce our blood pressure, promotes feelings of well-being, and is good for the heart.

A respected cardiologist, Dr. Stephen Yarnell, suggested in his seminar that, in order to have a healthy heart, it must be a happy one. He believes Type A and B personalities are not as impacting on our health as is anger. "That's the key," he stated, "dealing with and releasing anger, then choosing to be happy."

Dr. Steve Allen, Jr., passed out three small scarfs to all fifteen hundred of us, then proceeded to teach us to juggle. Juggling two silk scarfs wasn't bad, but three really messed me up. We practiced, dropped, and scooped fluttering scarfs, trying to get the idea the first evening. By Sunday afternoon, we were doing much better, so they trusted us with three marshmallows apiece. In a few minutes, boredom set it. Sitting near the front, I turned to see thousands of marshmallows being thrown stageward. For fifteen minutes, we were hit in the head, teeth, and legs with flying, puffy globs of sugar. What a unique and fun way to end a conference.

*Choosing the Amusing* is a delightful book by Marilyn Meberg, former Biola University English professor. Her book is filled with stories of wild abandonment to humor. She and her friend Luci Swindoll have shared experiences most people wouldn't dare to think, let alone do. I have asked her to speak at several events. On one occasion, prior to her address, we giggled all through the dinner. Even though Marilyn Meberg has gone through emotional pain, she has learned to laugh, and she practices Proverbs 17:22 (NAS): "A joyful heart is good medicine."

Hans Selye believed one of the best ways to reduce stress is to have a grateful heart. In other words, we need to quit our bellyaching and be thankful. "A tranquil heart is life to the body," says Proverbs 14:30 NAS. How true!

This thing called stress can be a roaring tiger out to destroy us. But we have a choice: We can be destroyed or we can take that baby by the the tail and sling it.

I'm getting better at it all the time.

# Insight for Growth

1. You look a bit stressed. Take five minutes and write down everything you can think of that causes stress. Now put it in categories under these headings: Surroundings, Guilt, Internal Stressors, Corporations, Relational Stressors, an Unforgiving Spirit, and Procrastination.

2. Rank the categories in order from the most stressful to the least stressful.

3. In what ways (physically, emotionally, and behaviorally) do you respond to these stressors?

4. Pick the top two stressors. Make a two-point plan of reduction for each one.

   a._____

      1)

      2)

   b._____

      1)

      2)

5. Put on some soothing music while doing a relaxation exercise for thirty minutes. At the conclusion, write down how you feel.

# 9

# RISK A NEW RELATIONSHIP? FORGET IT!

"You've got to be kidding! Count me out! No way!"

Granted, a new relationship is scary because we know the agony of rejection. We are not interested in going through that dark tunnel again. Yet we have a thread of hope that maybe someday we could have a happy and healthy marriage.

In order for that to occur, *we* must change. If we don't, we'll attract the same type of person and have a repeat performance. I have observed numerous second marriages in deep trouble because of a new partner who is very similar to a former spouse.

We need to scrutinize ourselves and give an honest appraisal following a marital breakup, then work on the areas that need growth. This takes time and guts, but it produces quality results.

Another safeguard is to learn about the male/female psychological distinctions. I'm sure you have noticed that men and women are very different.

Over and over in therapy I hear men say, "I'll never understand women." They are right. Neither will women fully comprehend men, but we can understand the dissimilar thought processes and learn to work within them. If we do, our relationships will be more fulfilling.

The following information regarding the psychological diversities of men and women is the *norm*, but it does not apply to everyone. For instance, some men will be able to express themselves emotionally while some women may operate more logically. Not only does the maleness and femaleness have a bearing but individual personality style and temperament must be considered as well.

## Male Logic Versus Emotions

A male spends most of his life operating from a logical stance. He has a "logic screen" through which all information is sorted. Whatever comes in is thought about from an analytical perspective. His logic is the filter through which experiences are organized. The intellect consumes most of his life. He is often more factually aligned and solution-oriented.

"Tell me what you think about the breakup of your marriage," I ask a male client.

"Well, I can't believe this is happening. I've always been a good provider for her and the kids. I thought she would be grateful. Obviously not. Why would a woman want to leave a beautiful home, an expensive car, charge accounts? Everything she's wanted, I've given her. For years, I've planned out our lives. We've taken great vacations. I have quite a financial portfolio going for us. I've done everything I know to make her happy, but she left."

Even though the male has great pain, it is vital he work through his thoughts about the situation first; he is usually quite uncomfortable dealing with emotions until he has come to grips with the intellectual.

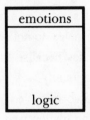

Above the logic is a much smaller area that houses the emotions. Men do not pop in and out of logic and emotion easily, for the emotions can be scary and unfamiliar. Thus, they are not readily expressed.

David W. Smith's book *The Friendless American Male* tells how our societal values have not allowed men to feel or express emotions as openly as women. Therefore, most male friendships function on a rather superficial level.

It is interesting how often men wish to see a woman therapist. Because men are competitive with one another and relate more around activities (e.g., golf), they often seek out a woman with whom they can share emotional secrets.

This can bring relational havoc to singles. Often a man will look for a woman confidante with whom he develops a friendship/ love bond. Quite often, the female will cross the line from friend/ love to being "in love." This is a very natural feminine response but is quite confusing to the male, particularly if he has stated up front that it was only friendship.

Generally, men are quite honest, but women believe they can change them. Consequently, when a woman learns a man is not in love with her, she may be very hurt, while he goes away scratching his head. *I told her at the beginning it was just friend-ship,* he thinks. And he's right.

Men tend to get the majority of their self-esteem needs met through their jobs. Females get most of theirs through love/home relationships. Therefore, males do not seek emotional bonding to the same degree as females because their self-worth needs are primarily being met vocationally.

Paul was a very eligible divorced man of God. He had a vibrant personality. During his ten years of singleness, Paul had dated numerous women on an exclusive-relationship basis and had been engaged several times.

At one point in therapy, I said, "Paul, have you ever been emotionally involved with any of these women?" A perplexed expression crossed his face, and his silence portrayed his deep thought. It seemed forever before he gave a reflective and delib-erate answer: "No. I guess I really haven't. That's probably why it has been so easy to break up and go on to someone new."

## Male Ego

All of this sounds as though men are incapable of emotional involvements. Not true. They have a great capacity.

When a male becomes emotionally involved with a woman (willing to commit himself to marriage), it can be uncomfortable and scary at first. When it is, he backs away. He goes into his comfort zone: his logic. He thinks it through. *Is this a good relationship? Is she really what I want? Do I want to be com-mitted to anyone?*

Committing himself emotionally means he is putting his ego on the line, and men have very fragile egos. Women mistakenly believe because a man is tall, muscular, and virile, he is just as strong inside. Nothing could be further from the truth. When a male trusts his fragile ego to a woman he loves, he has become vulnerable to her. The risk is great. She, in turn, has enormous power to destroy him. She can crush his ego as one would a raw egg.

A man whose wife has been unfaithful and left the marriage for a lover has great difficulty recovering, much more so than a woman when the situation is reversed. It is because of the fragility of the male ego.

This ego is a gift from God, and when a man offers it to a woman, she needs to give it great care.

## Spousal Ownership

There is also a sense of spousal "ownership" in men that is more intense than it is in women. It is not unusual for a man to refer to "my wife," even though she is remarried. Also, women clients who have been divorced for years have told me of remarried former husbands saying, "You're still my wife." It makes the letting-go process extremely difficult.

## Letting Go

Rick's sister called my office. "My brother's wife has left him for another man and he is threatening suicide. He called a suicide hot line and actually was put on hold. He's got a gun and says he's going to use it. I'm terrified. Can he get in to see you right now?"

He barely held it together in the waiting room, but once he hit my office, the deluge of tears began. His body shook with sobs and he could hardly talk. Finally, he said, "I just got too caught up in my job. It was everything to me. I really love my wife and

I wanted to make a good living for her and the kids, but I didn't give her enough attention and she's found somebody else. There's nothing to live for. I just want out. The pain's too much.''

Weeks into therapy, he was still distraught. My heart went out to him and I wondered, *Will he ever be able to deal with this and heal?*

About six weeks after the first visit, Rick marched into my office with an air of assurance accompanied by a steady, firm gait, pounded his fist on the arm of the chair, and roared, "I've had it! Enough of this garbage! I'm sick of the pain and I'm letting it go.'' He had left the emotional and gone back into his logic.

Bounding into my office two weeks later, smiles splashing all over his face, he announced, "I've met someone wonderful.''

Men have an uncanny ability to sever their emotions from their logic and act accordingly. "This just isn't working out for me,'' they reason and divorce their emotions. Often, though, they have not allowed adequate time to experience the full emotional impact. Because emotions are uncomfortable for them, they want to "get it over with fast.'' The letting-go process is too quick. They tend to repress their pain so they will feel better, rather than walk through the gut-wrenching experience and allow healing to occur slowly.

Men tend to get into new relationships too quickly. They want to get on with life and put pain in the past. Often they have multiple marriages. While I was talking with a Christian man recently, he remarked that he has been married four times.

"I dated most of my wives a short time—weeks—because I didn't want to take the time I needed to grow and heal. But six months ago, I married a wonderful person. We dated a year, with no sexual involvement. I finally got smart,'' he chuckled.

Finally, a male's God-given logic is a treasure, as are his emotions. He generally has a very developed logic but has difficulty living in the emotional part of himself. Yet David W. Smith's survey in *The Friendless American Male* found a man is attracted to people who will give him Acceptance, Empathy, Listening, Loyalty, Self-disclosure, and Compromise. Interesting—all of these needs are emotional.

## Female Emotions Versus Logic

As you have probably noted, a woman filters incoming stimuli through her emotional system. No matter how intelligent, professional, or logical she is, her sorting mechanism is through the emotions.

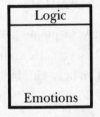

In therapy, I say, "Tell me how you feel." A woman needs to go into great detail about her feelings, using words that paint a vivid emotional picture. It may take months before she is capable or willing to logically look at her life. That's not to say she doesn't go in and out of logic easily, but she has a great need to express passionately.

Over and over I drum into women that if we live our lives by our emotions, we're in big trouble. It becomes a roller-coaster, out-of-control existence. Basing decisions on emotion rather than logic often brings disaster. Occasionally, we can operate from a "gut feeling," but not often. God gave us intellect and expects us to use it.

Sometimes men have a difficult time with women constantly expressing emotion. In an almost all-male counselors' meeting, I was unable to get a word in edgewise. After about an hour of trying to say something, I slammed my fist on the conference table and yelled, "Guys, it's my turn!" They looked stunned. *She's getting hysterical,* I envisioned them thinking. To that I retorted, "And I don't have my period." Gales of laughter broke up the meeting. Then they listened.

Because women get a good deal of their self-esteem needs met through love relations, they have a great ability to fantasize romantically.

## Fantasy

Ladies, remember back to junior high when your best girl-friend said, "Timmy likes you. He thinks you're cute." Now, Timmy could have been an ugly kid, but when you heard he was interested, he began to look much better. Soon, he was just adorable.

Then, fantasy took over—he was taking you out on a spectacular date (you had advanced to age sixteen).

"I've been in love since I first laid eyes on you. You're so beautiful, and to think you are mine. I just can't believe it. Marry me—now!" he murmured.

In the next flick, Tim (now a man) is gazing lovingly into your sparkling, excited eyes as you stand arm-in-arm before the minister. You timidly glance down at the most elegant white wedding gown ever made, then, tilting your chin upward, your gaze locks with that of the most dashing man in the whole world. Sigh!

Fantasy, for women, is romantic. It is also fun. Sometimes, though, it can get us into trouble because we visualize the relationship far beyond what is true. Our thoughts can hinder the natural progression and keep us from enjoying today.

## Emotional Involvement

In a dating relationship, a female can put on the brakes, promise herself, vow to God she *will not* get emotionally involved. But she does. A woman has a difficult time staying away from emotional involvement when she is interested in a man— sometimes even when she is not.

Because a man resists sharing intimate details with another male, he seeks out a woman.

"The moment we were introduced, there was an immediate attraction," Susan related to me in therapy. "We looked at each other and I thought, *Wow!* We have so much in common: sense of humor, vocation, values, upbringing. He's separated from his wife. This woman's a real slut. She's been involved in multiple affairs and is now living with a lover. He tells me all his secrets. I love it.

"Most of the time," she continued, "he tells me he's going to divorce that broad after what she's done to him for years. He thinks it's unfair and he deserves better and God doesn't expect him to live with it anymore. But the confusing part is that a couple of hours later, he'll tell me he wants the marriage to work out and says he just can't give her up."

"Susan," I responded, "watch out! You've traveled this road before and it's disastrous. You're going to get hurt. He needs a friend, and you're it. Yes, you are fascinated with each other, but it's not too likely there will ever be a dating relationship. Yes, you talk for hours, do things together, but it's not going any-where. Be smart—guard those emotions!''

On occasion, we talked about her relationship with Rick during therapy. One day about a year later, when Susan entered my office, I noticed a brightness about her.

"What's going on for you, Susan?" I questioned.

"Evidently, I've grown in my understanding of Rick's and my relationship, because I keep forgetting to tell you what's happen-ing," she answered. "You remember a few months back I took a promotion with another company. Well, Rick and I said our good-byes at the office. He's only called me once. Now that he's divorced, he can't be bothered with me. Guess he doesn't need me anymore. Boy, am I glad I listened to you. Operating from my logic rather than emotions saved me a lot of pain. I've de-cided to just write if off as a learning experience."

When a right-out-of-the-marriage (or right-out-of-a-long-term-relationship) man immediately reaches out to a woman, he usually needs *just a friend*. He wants a confidante, someone who will listen to and care for him. Yet the love bond grows as they share confidentially. Often a female steps over the line and is "in love." But when the male has reached a measure of healing and feels better about himself, he becomes logical and decides to go on with his life. He might meet a new woman and take off, forgetting all about his friend. She is hurt and can't understand how this could happen, after they have shared so much together.

It is vital that a woman understand this concept and be very cautious, especially if she appears strong and has her life to-gether. Often, a hurting man will be greatly attracted to her stability.

# Friendship

What I am going to say now will sound contradictory. A friendship is the foundation of a good dating relationship and a happy marriage. It takes lots of time to build, to learn about each other, to stop pretending, and to grow. A solid friendship is vital before romance ever enters the picture.

In the Rick-and-Susan situation, a needy man was desperately hurt and looking for comfort. In contrast, a male who is healthy and has had time to heal and grow after a long-term relationship, marital breakup, or spousal death is a good choice for friendship and perhaps future romantic involvement.

Since my marriage, I have loved two men. Both were friends for a year or more before romance entered the picture. During that year, we had time to know each other, observe each other's responses to people and situations, be honest, have fun, tell secrets, be good buddies, and grow without the entanglement of dating.

Now, the other side of the coin.

It has always been my fantasy (the feminine downfall) that when I meet *the one*, he will sweep me off my feet and everyone will sing, dance, and rejoice with us. Well, it happened.

He came along like a knight in shining armor, and I felt as though I were a princess as he carried me away amid flowers and the whispering of sweet nothings in my ear. It was glorious— while it lasted. Before long, I learned that this person who claimed I was the *only one* in his life was also carrying off several others on his snow-white steed.

Since a woman filters information emotionally, often she will not believe a man's logical statement if it is not what she wants to hear. She pretends it isn't so, that he really doesn't mean it, and she continues to fantasize about their relationship.

"I'm confused," Dan said in therapy. "I've told Debbie I think she's one terrific gal. We have so much fun together and I really enjoy her, but it's just friends with me. I really wish it could be more, but it can't. Someday she's going to make some guy a great wife. I've tried to be honest with her."

Debbie and Dan do have a great time and are bonded. But she was probably thinking, *I know Dan is just out of his marriage, but we really do have something special. I'm different from his wife and all those other women. One day he'll wake up and realize he's in love with me and we'll get married. I just know it's going to happen.* Debbie keeps on dreaming.

"I just don't understand why Debbie keeps wanting more, when I've told her we're friends," Dan reported. "Frankly, I'm feeling trapped. I think I need to go on with my life."

Dan soon began a new dating relationship, and Debbie was crushed.

A word to the wise: If a man tells you he just wants to be friends and doesn't want to get serious or marry, *believe him*!

The first day I laid eyes on Paul, I thought, *Oh, my goodness, what a hunk*. He later told me he had similar feelings. His marriage had produced three boys but was rather short-lived. I always sensed he had not fully let go, even though the marriage had been over for several years.

Early in our friendship, Paul said, "Jeenie, I don't ever want to remarry. I can't face it again."

After a year, our friendship blossomed into romance. With a look full of tenderness, Paul often said, "Jeenie, if I could just wake up and already be married to you, it would be great. But I just can't go through with it."

"I know," I responded. "I've never counted on it. You told me from the beginning and I believed you."

As females, we have a fantasy that we will be so unique, we can get men to change their minds about friendship and marriage. Occasionally, this may occur, but the chances are slim. It is more healthy to listen to what they tell us at the beginning and act accordingly—enjoy what we have for this season of life. Then we can have wonderful and loving memories rather than frustration and/or pain.

The relationship with Paul spanned four years and was filled with honesty, hours of talking, and lots of fun.

Sitting on a park bench, I stuck my fingers into his ice tea glass and dug out the ice. "Hey, Paul, have you ever had an ice-spitting contest?" I asked. He looked at me as though I were crazy. "Okay, see that trash can over there?" I continued. "We're going to see who can hit it the most times." With that, I whirled a piece of ice out of my mouth directly into the barrel. "Top that," I said. Giggling, we took turns spitting until the ice was gone. I made it every time. He didn't—not even once.

"Promise me you will never spit ice with anyone else. This is our commitment to each other," he grinned.

Over a year later, I sleepily picked up the phone late one evening and gasped, "Paul! I can't believe it! How good to hear from you."

"Now, you haven't been in any ice-spitting contests with anyone, have you?" Paul replied. "Remember, we promised."

Even though the romantic relationship is long over, the bonding and friendship still remains. Friendship is the foundation for meaningful connections and is primary groundwork for marriage.

## Communication Differences

Men and women generally express themselves while operating through their filtering system (logical or emotional). As an example, the washing machine breaks down. After it's all over, both the male and female give details to a friend.

Female:     "It was awful. Water was spurting all over the kitchen. Soap was seeping out the top and running down the sides and front. Wouldn't you know, I'd just spent an hour yesterday cleaning and polishing it. I just couldn't believe it. It sounded like *chugga, chugga,* and *whish, whish,* then it gurgled. I tried to get my former husband on the phone and he was in a meeting, so I had him called out. He screamed at me, and I cried. Well, I unplugged it and leafed through the yellow pages to get someone to come look at it. The repairman was real nice, even kind of cute. While he was fixing the washer, I mopped up the floor. I decided to wait until later to wax it. He said the machine was in real bad shape, and it cost me a lot of money. Well, there goes that dress I'd had my eye on."

Male:       "The washer went out. The guy charged me a hundred and twenty bucks. I could have fixed it myself if I'd had time."

In the same scenario, the man tells only the pertinent facts (logic), whereas the female describes every detail with inordinate emotion.

## His Needs/Her Needs

In working with thousands of couples, clinical psychologist Dr. Willard F. Harley pinpointed five basic needs for women and five for men. His book *His Needs, Her Needs* is one I consistently recommend to clients in therapy. Dr. Harley contends that when a spouse is willing to meet his or her partner's needs, the relationship will be healthier. The list is in order of priority.

*Her Needs:* Affection, Conversation, Honesty and Openness, Financial Support, Family Commitment

*His Needs:* Sexual Fulfillment, Recreational Companionship, An Attractive Spouse, Domestic Support, Admiration

Because males and females are unalike psychologically, they enter the dating scene dissimilarly.

## Relationship Phases

*Everybody Needs Somebody Sometime* by Gerald L. Dahl talks in great detail about five phases of relationships: Attraction, Testing, Commitment, Maintaining, and Ending. After working with hundreds of single adults, I concur with Dahl's thinking. However, I have some correlating thoughts about Attraction, Testing, Commitment, Sexuality, and Closure.

### *Attraction*

The pumpkins greeted us with wide, semitoothless smiles as candles blinked from their eyes. The getups at the party were wild, unique, crazy, and ingenious. Now it was time to judge the costumes and guess who was wearing them. One guest stymied everyone. The mute hunchback defied all the guesses and answered with a back-and-forth shake of the head. Who was he?

*Hmmm,* I thought as I looked at his hands. "That's Jack!" I announced.

"How could you tell?" the others responded?

"Well, I'm aware of people's hands. Those are Jack's," I said. In fact, I've identified numerous mystery guests by observing their hands.

All of us have a variety of physical characteristics and personal qualities to which we are drawn. They stand out to us and we are pulled toward the person who possesses them. Perhaps it is eyes, an enticing laugh, a unique walk, an alluring smell, or a certain body type that captivates us.

When we first met at a singles party, I was attracted to a certain man. He didn't notice me. A year later, we spent an evening with a group playing cards and immediately began dating.

"Remember the party where we met?" he asked one night. "Well, you were very appealing to me, but I thought you were with someone else, so I let it go. I watched you and really liked the way you moved."

"What do you mean—moved?" I asked.

"I'm not sure, but it was different and I liked it," he responded.

Interesting. I still don't know how I "move" because however it is, it is normal for me, but someone found it unusual and appealing.

Because we are such different personalities and temperaments, there is a wide range of qualities that attract us to others.

Even though women are physically attracted, they are more captivated by other traits: personality, intelligence, and other innate qualities of a person. This occurs because women operate more from their emotional/intuitive level, and one of their greatest needs is for affection and conversation.

Men, on the other hand, are physically attracted, which goes along with their great need for sexual fulfillment. They, too, find other qualities alluring, but the physical one is generally prominent. Also, seldom will a man have a woman friend in whom he is not interested physically.

Attraction crosses gender lines. We become friends with those people who appeal to us. On occasion, I have approached a person and said, "You seem like someone I'd like to get to know. It seems you are fun, sincere, and honest." A big grin crosses his or her face, we begin a conversation, and sometimes we really do become friends.

A woman once said to me, "I've watched you and really admire you. I think we could be friends." I thought about it and glowed for days. I felt important and special.

How much we need to reach out and be a bit vulnerable and honest with our thoughts and feelings.

## Testing

Perhaps testing a friendship/relationship sounds very clinical, calculating, and manipulative. No one is thrilled about being scrutinized. But as human beings, we automatically test. It helps protect us from undue pain and rejection. It enables us to make wise relational choices. Having been attracted to unhealthy relationships, it was very difficult for me to come to the point of believing I even had a choice.

Several years ago, I slowly became more aware of my addiction to unhealthy relationships. Digging back into childhood, I scrutinized friendships. To my astonishment, I realized the enormity of the addiction, for I had been consistently "dumped" by friends. It had become such a pattern in my life that it was now normal.

As I began to methodically deal with my dependency needs and compulsion, I contended, "There really is an option as to whom I let into my life. I can select. I have a choice as to whether or not I want this friendship." This was a tremendous breakthrough for me. In the past, I did not believe myself worthy of having any say-so. Since I felt ineligible for acceptance and love, I took what came—including multiple rejections.

Friendship is a two-way street. It is important that both persons give to the relationship. At times, one may give more, but there needs to be an equality over the long haul.

There are takers and there are givers, and they always seem to find each other. Because of my compulsion, I have had a lot of takers pass through my life. As soon as their needs are met, they split, looking for greener pastures. Those types of friendships are based primarily on the ability of the giver to meet needs. Because the giver is dependent and emotionally needy, it is easy to get sucked in. It feels good for a time, but eventually, the giver ends up hurt and rejected.

Example: "I've really missed you," you say with a smile. "When can we get together again?"

"Oh, wow, my life is just too full and busy. Let me take a look here." Looking at the appointment book, the "friend" muses, "Well, it seems I'll have an hour on the sixteenth. I know it's five weeks away, but you know how it is. Look, why don't you drive out my way—it would be a lot easier for me."

"Well, okay, that would be fine," you return.

Any hints slap you in the face in this illustration? The enslavement is profound. Need is surpassing good sense. It is time to change.

A more healthy response would be, "I really want our friendship, but I'm getting the feeling you're not sure you want to squeeze me into your schedule. That's not what I want. If you wish to get together, give me a call. We'll see what we can work out that will be fair to both of us.''

This type of response is honest as well as self-respecting. Takers who do not regard óthers must be called on it.

Each of us should have one friend we could telephone in the middle of the night, if the need arose. Givers have a difficult time asking for help or allowing their needs to be met. Takers, on the other hand, don't give it a second thought.

Ann was a taker. She was widowed and depended on her longtime friend Bev. Bev was up and out early in the morning; her work schedule was demanding and hectic. However, she was always available to listen and care. Almost every morning, Ann would call around half-past six for a short chat that often turned into a half-hour conversation. Bev couldn't bring herself to cut it short or even to ask Ann not to call. "What am I going to do?" she asked me one day in counseling.

"Call Ann early this evening," I responded. "Tell her, 'Ann, I know it's very difficult for you right now. I love you and want to be available. However, it's inconvenient when you call each morning. I leave late for work, drive like crazy, get into the middle of commuter traffic, and start the day in a bad mood. I will not be able to talk to you in the morning, so please do not call. We can still see each other and talk on the phone, but it will need to be more limited.' ''

Ann was furious! She jettisoned out of the friendship like a rocket and found someone else. Later, Bev heard through the grapevine that Ann was saying, "You just can't count on Bev. She got all bent out of shape because I called her a couple of times. She's so busy, you know. No time for anyone. I don't know where she gets off acting like this."

Typical response.

Sometimes, the change is not as drastic and the friendship can still exist but at a more casual, less intimate level. If we realize a person is a taker, we need to be cautious as to how much emotional and time involvement we can allow.

Testing tends to be an up-and-down process, with both parties ascertaining whether the friendship will meet mutual needs. If the testing goes on for years, however, something is amiss. It would appear that one or both are unwilling to make a commitment.

## *Commitment*

Most male/female relationships never get to this stage because it involves risk, self-disclosure, vulnerability, and the possibility of being hurt. Committing oneself is difficult.

"I met this super woman a year ago and she's a real fox," a patient grinned. "We started out as friends and it kind of went from there. The more I've gotten to know her, the better she looks. She treats me like a king. We have a lot of fun and tell each other our secrets. She's one person I can really trust. I couldn't ask for anyone better. She beats my ex by a long shot." His eyes were dancing as his smile zipped from ear to ear.

*Hmmm,* I thought, *there's more to all this.* Leaning back into my office chair, I said, "But?"

Cocking his head, Sam became more sober. "Yeah, but," he replied. "You're right. There's a big *but*. After my wife ran off with her lover and left me with the kids, I promised myself I'd never again trust a woman. They seem wonderful—until you're married. It changes. I just can't take the chance of ever being that crushed again. Nothing is worth it. Nothing."

"So," I responded, "you're willing to block out happiness so you can keep yourself protected from pain. Is that really what you want—safety at any cost?"

"No," Sam answered, "but I'm just too scared to go for it."

Rejection puts the brakes on divorced people. They are cautious, less trusting, and sometimes scared to death of pledging themselves to another person—forever.

By contrast, another client came to me for counseling after the death of his wife of forty years. He, too, went through enormous pain and emotional upheaval. About six months into therapy, I noticed he had removed his wedding ring.

"Allen, I see you've taken off your wedding band," I remarked.

"Uh-huh," he answered. "It's time. In fact, I've been going to a group for widows and widowers and met some nice women. I've taken several of them out for dinner. But I have my eye on one. She's a real catch. I think we're good for each other." By the end of the year, Allen had married this lovely woman. Unlike Sam, Allen wasn't hindered by rejection and could more easily commit to another relationship.

Commitment is a verbal statement of the heart. Say it! It allows us to be ourselves, reinforces self-esteem, gives rise to honesty, allows us to spend quality time together, enables us to build memories, and brings encouragement and nurturing. The fewer the conditions, the greater the commitment.

A word of caution: The commitment stage should not be entered too quickly, as people need adequate time to test and sort out issues.

Max and Helen "fell in love" the moment their eyes met. Hands touched, hearts palpitated, sweat glands secreted. Their relationship was God-ordained, or so they thought. "Why wait?" they cooed, looking longingly into each other's eyes. There certainly was no reason when they were "meant to be." They dated two weeks just to be sure.

Four months later, they were just as certain they were not to be married. Each of them filed for the second divorce in a year.

Perhaps they could have had a healthy marriage if they had taken a year to work on it or, at worst, mutually elected to break up prior to marriage.

Commitment takes a great deal of quality preparatory time. It is also an ongoing process, not a one-time thing.

## *Sexuality*

We are made by God to be sexual beings. When we commit to a person, it is a natural desire to have sex.

Formerly marrieds naturally progressed from the beginnings of romantic expression to sexual intercourse with their spouses. They enjoyed the freedom of sexual demonstration.

When people are separated or divorced, the channel for expression is gone, but not the desire. For many, it becomes more intense. It's like being on a diet: all we can think about is food.

I have heard numerous well-meaning, godly pastors of singles give their "Stay Away From Sex" talks, then go home to their wives. They are biblically correct, and I wholeheartedly concur, but they have no idea how difficult it is to keep the sexual faucet turned off when one is dying for a drink. Thus, sex becomes a complex issue for the "single again."

We must come to grips with our sexuality and make decisions accordingly. Harold Ivan Smith's book *A Part of Me Is Missing* is an excellent resource. In it, he outlines human needs and spiritual principles. I highly recommend giving careful thought to his stance.

In each of us, there is an innate need to be close to someone, to be loved unconditionally, and to feel accepted and free enough to be transparent. This can only be achieved by a slow bonding process. It takes time to become intimate.

Often singles try to fill an emotional void by becoming instantly intimate through sexual expression, but it just doesn't work. Psychologists state that when there is early sexual involvement, intimacy is achieved at a low and unsatisfying level, if at all.

## Closure

When a relationship begins, something in us is born. When it ends, something dies.

Few of us have lifelong friends. Rarely do people carry grammar school buddies into adulthood. As life changes and takes on new characteristics, new friends emerge, and many older relationships come to an end. There is, however, a right and a wrong way to bring about closure.

Most relationships are not concluded; some just drift to an end and others are ripped apart by anger, hurt, and misunderstanding.

Gerald L. Dahl's book *Everybody Needs Somebody Sometime* had great impact on me regarding the right kind of closure. As I allowed this concept to permeate my thinking, I vowed never again to end a relationship without doing it in a kind, honest manner. In thinking through the process, I have also chosen to go back and deal with some former friendships using Dahl's procedure.

Have you ever heard yourself saying, "Listen, your moving will have absolutely no bearing on our friendship. We'll write and call each other all the time. After all, friends are forever and nothing will change. We'll keep in touch."

All the time you both knew it was unlikely, even though your motives were good. Maybe there were even a few phone calls and a note or two, but as time went on, it became "out of sight, out of mind." When the friend would pop into your mind several months later, you would think, *I must give her a call.* When you didn't, you felt guilty. Before long, you didn't give her a second thought—or experience guilt.

Dahl suggests that the *first* step in closure is to recognize the end has come. Talk about it honestly with the person and state the reasons.

Shelly and I had been friends for years. Her listening ear was always accessible during the dark days of my separation and divorce. Now she was moving, and instead of a fifteen-minute drive, it would be over two hours.

"We've been friends for such a long time," I said over lunch. "Even though there will always be a love bond between us, the reality is that we just won't be in touch all that much after you move."

*Second,* express how the friend has nurtured you. Be specific— use illustrations.

"Shelly, I can never fully verbalize how dear you are to me. Sitting over coffee, tears splashing on the tablecloth, I sobbed the story of my broken marriage to you. Your hands reached across the table, grasped mine, and held on tight. You cried with me and never offered advice, just cared and really loved me. When the pain overwhelmed me, you held me in your arms and comforted me. You've been there when I needed you—not only in the sad times but also the times when we laughed so hard and acted so crazy we were afraid they'd throw us out of the restaurant. I treasure these memories."

*Third,* the expression of love is usually returned.

"Thank you, Jeenie. That's precious of you. I'm also very grateful for your friendship. You've listened to me when I've been angry, sad, and disappointed. Remember the job I wanted so badly? They told me I was the top candidate. It was a big move up with a lucrative salary, and I'd worked hard for years, hoping to someday have the promotion. Then they very suddenly gave it to an outsider. I was devastated. It was so unfair. You empathized with me, built up my ego, and told me what a good worker I am and that any company would be proud to have me. With your encouragement, I explored other positions and was offered an even better one. You believed in me. I love you and am so grateful for our friendship, for the times we've had alone as well as with our families.''

When the ending is honest and loving, the relationship memories are pleasant. Conversely, when it is not, the recollections tend to be negative, and the scenario is often quite different.

"Lou was a hunk—a holy one," Susie confided in a therapy session. "Fun, too. He often stopped by my office for a short chat. On more than one occasion when I was away from my desk, he delighted me by leaving a single rose he'd picked outside with a note attached. We had a lot in common and really enjoyed each other.

" 'I've decided to become a dentist,' he voiced one day. After a few months, he announced, 'I've been accepted at a New York medical school and I leave next week.' Then he left. No goodbye, no note, no call. I couldn't believe it. After digging a bit, I found his address and wrote a short message. He never responded.

"Before long, I had forgotten the good times and only remembered the way he left. I felt disappointed, hurt, and angry.

"Five years later, I walked into an adjoining office and was startled to see him. He had come by to visit one of my male co-workers. We exchanged a "Hi, how are you?" He gave me a superficial hug and I left with the bad taste of an old rejection in my mouth.''

How sad for Susie. She and Lou once had something special, but the way it ended all but eliminated pleasant memories.

If friendships die without kind termination, negative thoughts tend to replace memories of the good times. However, the friendships we sincerely and carefully close become forever.

## The Good News Is . . .

We can love again, if we are willing to become vulnerable and risk. The more we know about ourselves and the opposite sex, as well as the stages of a relationship, the better equipped we are to get out there and give it a chance. Who knows, God may have someone for us!

# Insight for Growth

1. Males and females think radically differently. What surprises you the most about the opposite sex?

2. Your former spouse is sitting on the other side of a one-way glass. Since your ex cannot see or hear you, tell him/her one way you could have acted differently had you been aware of the logical versus emotional screens.

3. In opposite-sex or same-sex friendships, at what stage are you most often stuck? Is there one that frightens you?

4. Think through your ideas about your sexuality. Write a guideline you wish to uphold. Be specific.

# 10

# LEARNING BY WAITING

Sooner or later, God takes all of His children into "the room." My turn came in 1976. I stepped into a blinding glare, then experienced an unsettling feeling as the stark whiteness seemed to slap me in the face. Timidly, I searched for windows and doors, but there were none. The room was empty—no chair, bed, table, or pictures on the walls. As a sense of anxiety encompassed me, I bolted for the door. There was no knob. Reality hit. My heart pounded; beads of perspiration collected on my forehead. My hands were cold and clammy. Terrifying thoughts thundered through my mind: *I can't escape. I'm trapped. There's no way out unless someone opens the door.* This is God's waiting room.

As pampered human beings, our tendency is to run through painful times as fast as possible. We want to get them over with and get back to normal, but just the opposite promotes healing. It is vital that we *walk* through the process. Because our tendency is to stampede toward health, I believe God places us in His waiting room.

A separation/divorce, in my thinking, dumps us headlong into the waiting-room experience. Even though we are in this room against our will, we have options. Only we can decide what we will do during this season of time.

The natural tendency is to bang our heads on the floor, cry, pummel the wall with clenched fists, scream, beat the door, yell, promise . . . yet we remain in the room. Only God can open the door—when He's ready.

As much as I despise this concept, I'm convinced there is no growth without pain. You are probably thinking, *Hey, I'd gladly give up growth in exchange for a pain-free existence.* So would most people. But with hurting comes the opportunity to someday enjoy the freedom of a joyous life and evolve into the person God has chosen us to be. Then, in retrospect, we can be grateful for the lessons learned during the dark times.

## The Waiters

A few years back, best-selling author Charles Swindoll dealt expertly with the topic of waiting. In a sermon, he cited biblical illustrations of those who experienced long and tedious times of waiting for God to answer their cries.

God promised Abraham he would have a son. Sarah got anxious (she was far past her childbearing years) and decided to help out God. She talked Abraham into impregnating Hagar, and Ishmael was born. Abraham's union with Hagar caused a whirlwind of trouble that still exists today between the Jews and Arabs. Finally, God gave Abraham and Sarah a son, Isaac. The wait, however, was a long one. No wonder they lost hope.

When I read the story of Noah building his ark, the great flood, and the subsequent destruction of mankind, it seemed it happened rather quickly. How amazed I was to learn that Noah was hammering on that ark for 120 years before it rained. I can hear his neighbors jabbing him: "Hey, Noah, why are you building that boat? We've never had rain before, and it won't happen. Why don't you give up!" But Noah kept building and believing God— for 120 years. Now, that's a wait!

Moses—the young Egyptian prince, raised in wealth, viewed with prestige, well educated—was exiled by God in the wilderness forty years. He did not become the great deliverer and leader of Israel until he had served his time.

My favorite is Joseph. This pompous, spoiled lad was sold by his own kin to some passersby and landed in Egypt. Soon he found himself owned by Potiphar, captain of the royal guard. Now, Potiphar's wife had an eye for handsome and virile young men, and Joseph fit the bill. Because he resisted her, she had to resort to trickery. Believing Joseph had attempted to rape his wife, Potiphar had him put into prison. Unjustly accused, Joseph waited (yet excelled) in prison for years. But God did not forget. Because of his willingness to be faithful to God and continue to trust Him, he became the envied ruler under Pharaoh and experienced the grandeur of the Egyptian empire.

## Positive Versus Negative Waiting

My pastor searched my face as I said, "My husband is going to leave me. I haven't a choice about the continuation of my marriage, but I do about my response. Believe me, I'm not about to go through all this pain for nothing. There's no way I want to end up bitter. When it's over, I intend to be a far better person."

While waiting, we can take steps that will equip us for life "outside." Even in the most down times we can be productive, but it entails large doses of discipline. It is vital, however, to take responsibility for our lives. If we want life to be good, then we make good things happen. The more positive things we do for ourselves, the more satisfying and fulfilling life will be. When we do the preparatory work, we allow God to bring miracle opportunities. He cannot give us anything for which we are not equipped.

The morning sun streamed through the window, caressing a face swollen from a night of tears. Even through the pain, disappointment, and terror, there was a warming ray of hope.

My husband had walked out of the marriage. During the stillness and aloneness of the dark hours, I read Robert H. Schuller's book *Move Ahead With Possibility Thinking*. It jarred my being with the concept that I could *choose* to look at the possibilities rather than the disaster. As God began bringing ideas into my mind, I wrote them down. In looking over the notes, I discovered several names of key people who could guide me with their wisdom.

Then I lost my list. I hunted through the entire bedroom, but it was nowhere to be found. Now came the job of rewriting the list. My mind was blank. I knew there were three names, but I could remember only one—an author/lecturer who was a professor at my alma mater.

While reading Robert Schuller's book through that long, black night, a thought came to me: perhaps I could do some manuscript typing. Realizing the author was a busy professional, I doubted she had time to do her own typing. I also thought I could complete the last semester of my master's degree in counseling. If I didn't, I would be sunk looking for a job.

Then I began to feel stupid. I wasn't sure how to present my proposal, so I procrastinated—for weeks.

The thought would not leave, so I wrote a brief note to the woman and enclosed my telephone number. To be honest, I did it to get the Lord off my back. He kept bringing it up.

When I answered the insistent ring of the telephone, the professor began, "Jeenie, I already have several people to type manuscripts. However, I need someone to do my mail. By any chance, do you take shorthand?"

"Yes, I do," I responded.

By the end of the week, I began working with her and continued nearly four years—long after I had a full-time counseling position. We developed a friendship that was honest, caring, fun, and delightful. God placed her in my life at a time when I needed employment and a support system.

Meanwhile, back to the lost-list episode.

My husband left in March, and by June I was ready to do fieldwork for my master's degree. One requirement was met by working in a large mental hospital in Los Angeles County (a book in itself). The last assignment was to be a counselor in a school setting.

Racking my brain for a possibility, I remembered a high school principal under whom my husband had served. Even though I had met him only a few times, this man and I had a rapport.

*I'll call him,* I thought. Then my heart began to race as I practiced what I would say. Would he remember me? Would he have an internship available? Would he even care?

His secretary put him through. "Jeenie," the principal exclaimed, "I've been thinking about you and wondering how you're doing."

When I explained my need, he responded, "Hey, the red carpet is rolled out for you, and I'll give you anything you need."

He assigned a fine man I had met previously to be my fieldwork supervisor. He was a Christian and became my encourager and mentor.

Wouldn't you know, six months later I found my list! It was between the mattress and box spring—a perfect place for a list.

Curiously, I looked at the names of the two missing persons. One was the principal. The other was the fieldwork supervisor.

It was as if God said, *See, Jeenie, I really* do *have your life planned. You can count on Me to guide you, to love you, and to make provisions for your needs.*

Seldom do we see a miracle in retrospect, but God allowed me this privilege. It gave me courage to go on and to trust Him implicitly. At no time in my life have I seen as many miracles as during my divorce process. I feel strongly that God gives us a miracle only when it is needed. When life is beyond our control, we can fully count on Him.

In January 1976, I began a small spiral notebook, which I now call my Miracle Book. Each month, I ask God for several specific things. When a request is answered, I circle it and date it. Most of the items in my Miracle Book are circled with a "yes" written above them. There are others that are still awaiting answers. A few have "no" penned beside them. My Miracle Book is now into Volume II.

Sometimes when I'm discouraged, angry, and disappointed, I say, "God, You *never* do anything for me. You *always* do all these wonderful things for other people—people who don't even deserve it as much as I do." When I finally stop complaining and having a pity party, I leaf through my Miracle Book. As tears of shame mix with those of gratitude, I again realize the enormity of His love, confident I can trust Him with my life.

## Blending Together

Romans 8:28 KJV states, "And we know that all things work together for good to them that love God, to them who are the called according to his purpose."

This verse is quoted often and glibly to people who are experiencing trauma. Evidently the "comforter" feels this is really going to do it—to make a suffering person see the light, feel super, be spiritual, forget, and get on with life. It doesn't.

When the man stumbled into my office, his bloodshot eyes showed his distress. He had been a pastor. Now his future was bleak.

"When I married Ann, I really felt God wanted us together. There was no one I had ever met I could love more. She was just what I'd always wanted," he sobbed. A distant look appeared on his rugged face and softly he continued, "She was just too beautiful. Every man wanted her, and she could never resist."

In deep thought, we sat in silence. I watched the agony of his soul escaping through his sad, brown eyes. Finally, he spoke. "You know, one of my parishioners quoted Romans 8:28 to me. I couldn't believe he would do that to me when my pain is so intense and life is hopeless and dark. That verse was not what I wanted to hear. How can things be working for good? That's ridiculous. I don't believe it! Furthermore, I don't want to hear any spiritual platitudes, especially when he has not experienced my kind of pain. I felt like telling him to just get off my back!" Thinking about my pastor client a few days later, I asked God to help me look at this Scripture differently.

The illustration of baking a cake from scratch came to me. Picture it with me.

Selecting a large bowl, a wooden spoon, a glass measuring cup, and a recipe, the arduous process begins. The first ingredient is a cup of shortening. Now, let's say I decided to take a big spoonful and pop it into my mouth. Yuck! It would take about two seconds before I began to spit it out, which would be no small effort because the stuff would spread distasteful grease all over my teeth and gums. Hardly a taste treat.

Next, the recipe calls for two cups of sugar. Dumping a whole bunch of sugar in my mouth, mixed with grease, would be terrible. There is no way it would stay put. Mary Poppins' idea of a spoonful of sugar to make the medicine go down is not the same as two cups by a long shot.

Then the recipe calls for two raw eggs. In the movie *Rocky*, Sylvester Stallone certainly had no trouble sliding raw eggs into his mouth and letting them slither down his throat. But I do. The thought sickens me.

Now the flour—three sifted full-to-the-brim cups. I can hardly picture putting even a tablespoon of that into my mouth. Flour sticks, and the more it is dampened with saliva, the worse it gets.

Baking soda, salt, and baking powder are then added. Not exactly a gourmet delight for the palate.

Finally comes the chocolate. Yum! To a chocoholic, this ingredient sounds wonderful. But to my surprise, it is bitter.

Each of these ingredients by itself is distasteful. However, when they are blended together, beaten, and baked in a hot oven, they become a mouth-watering treat. A cake emerges that smells delectable and has a taste to match.

So many of the events in our lives are distasteful in themselves. There is separation, divorce, death, rejection, job change, home loss, lowering of status, financial difficulties, and problems with children. But God takes problematic events and begins to slowly and deliberately *blend* them together. "For God blends all things together for good . . ." (my paraphrase). As we allow Him to work in our lives, we can, in His time, emerge into beautiful creations. He can turn disasters into blessings.

Recently I ran into my former pastor client. "Jeenie," he laughed as he swooped me up in a hug. Those once sad eyes now twinkled with excitement. Jubilance danced across his face as he said, "You won't believe my life! God has turned it all around. He sent me a wonderful wife. She's involved with me in a new ministry, and we have a great marriage. I used to envy your outlook on life. When I'd leave counseling, I would wonder if I, too, could ever be happy again. It all seemed so impossible. But it happened. The pain is gone and I'm so grateful to God. He really does work things out for good."

## Not in Vain

Much of life is spent waiting for answers to problems over which we seem to have no control. However, we can choose how we will *respond* to these difficulties, and when the waiting time has elapsed, we emerge. Our exit is similar to that of a caterpillar encased in the cocoon who struggles, endeavoring to break out, and eventually flies with grace, soaring upward on majestic, multicolored wings.

A beautiful verse, Isaiah 40:31 RSV, says, "But they who wait for the Lord shall renew their strength, they shall mount up with wings like eagles, they shall run and not be weary, they shall walk and not faint."

Even though we wait, we wait not in vain but with hope.

# Insight for Growth

1. Describe your feelings while you are in God's waiting room (e.g., fear, disappointment, anger, frustration, panic, anxiety, bitterness, deep hurt, and so on).

2. What negative things are you doing to yourself that are hindering your healing?

3. Name two productive things you can do. When (exact date) will you begin?

4. State one request you have of God.

# 11

# THIS THING CALLED TRUST

"Come on, you can't be serious. I'm supposed to trust?" you mutter.

"Yep, you've got it!" I retort. "It's hard. Sometimes it seems nearly impossible, but the payoffs are dynamite."

Take Hezekiah, my hero. He was quite a king. His greatness ensued because of his trust in Jehovah God. He lived in the days when good kings were few and far between.

His kingdom was thriving, people loved him, life seemed grand—until he got *the* letter. (Ever get one of those?) It happened to be from his enemy, King Sennacherib of Assyria. Big *S* was a mean dude—out to "clean Hezekiah's clock." He had already seized all the fortified cities of Judah and now was determined to take Jerusalem. This man wanted blood! He had a way of expressing threats on parchment that scared the sandals off Hezekiah.

Terrified Hezekiah read the letter, then he:

1. went to the house of the Lord
2. spread it out before Jehovah
3. prayed like crazy

In fact, most of chapter 37 in Isaiah is devoted to Hezekiah's petition and God's response. As he prayed, the Lord comforted him through the prophet by saying, "For I will defend this city to save it for My own sake and for My servant David's sake" (Isaiah 37:35 NAS).

God came through! He sent the angel of the Lord through the Assyrian camp as the snoring of the soldiers shook the tents and killed all 185,000 of them!

Needless to say, King Sennacherib woke up, gazed in speechless horror at the massacre, jumped on his horse in one bound, and hightailed it home, grateful to be alive.

## Give the Problem to God

Hezekiah's plan in the face of disaster is one I've adopted. He went to the house of the Lord, spread his problem out, and prayed. What healthy actions.

At times I feel a foreboding fear, depression, or low-grade anxiety hanging over me and there is nothing I can do to change the situation. Most of the time I make a beeline to my place of prayer (the Lord's house). Kneeling at my bed, I lay it out before God. Sometimes I actually write it out; other times I verbalize my fears. I go into great detail about the problem, telling the Lord exactly what I fear and how I feel. At the conclusion, I give it to God. "Father, this is too big for me. I'm not capable of handling it. So, it's Yours. You are a God of miracles, and I need one now."

During the day, anxious thoughts may still permeate my mind.

As soon as I'm aware of them, I shoot them back to the Lord. "I gave this problem to You this morning, Father, and I choose not to think about it. It's Your problem now." Then, I deliberately change my thoughts and/or do something else. Again, each time my mind returns to the thoughts and fear erupts, I return it to God. This may happen hundreds of times a day at first, but as each day progresses, it lessens and I become stronger. My trust is strengthened.

Only when we are able to relax our clenched fists and give up whatever we are hanging on to (whether it is fear or a collapsing marriage) is God able to give us anything better. As we open our hands, we now have room to receive God's gift. I wonder if we tie the hands of God to work in our behalf when we refuse to let go. How many good things we have probably missed because we are unwilling to surrender to God's will.

When we disengage, we allow God to come through for us. And He does!

# Insight for Growth

1. Worry and anxious thoughts are etched in ever-deepening lines on your face. Write down the one thing that terrifies you the most.

2. Close your eyes. Wrap your hands tightly around this frightening thought. Clench your fists. Hold on.

3. Slowly open your fists until your palms are exposed. Say a prayer:

   Dear God, I give _____ to you. I'm terrified, but I'm going to count on You for a miracle. Here it is, Lord, take it. It's Yours.

# 12

# A MESSENGER FROM GOD

It had been a good retreat. The singles were responsive to my workshop, and I was feeling warmed by the fact God had chosen to use me. Coming down the mountain was a delight. I cracked the car windows so I could feel the breeze, bask in the afternoon sun, and smell the aroma of pine. The clouds were white mounds that looked as if huge cotton balls had been thrown by God into the azure sky.

I glanced at my watch. It was 3:30 P.M. "Good," I sighed. "I should be home by five o'clock."

Merging into light Saturday freeway traffic, I glanced into my side mirror as well as looking behind me. In the next moment, something caused me to hit my head, and I was knocked into a semiconscious state. (Weeks later, I read the police report. They were unable to determine what caused the accident. My belief is that I was hit by another vehicle.)

I could feel the careening of my car and hear the squealing of brakes. It seemed my vehicle was lurching all over the roadway.

My eyes were tightly closed, and I was unable to open them. It was as though I were desperately trying to awaken from a dream but was unable to do so. In an urgent attempt to right the situation, grabbing the steering wheel in both hands, I turned sharply to the right. "There!" I exclaimed. My foggy mind reasoned, *Now I've fixed it. It's okay.* I then slid into unconsciousness.

Awakening thirty minutes later, I couldn't believe the disaster. My car was entwined in eucalyptus trees at the bottom of a ravine. A crowd had gathered on the edge, staring down at the accident. Looking around my car, I saw that the roof was ripped apart, the windows smashed, and the inside nearly demolished. In physical shock, I kept repeating, "Oh, my God. Oh, my God."

After viewing the damage of the car, I numbly looked down at my body. There was no blood. *Thank God,* I thought. My shoes were off and I was sitting on the passenger's side with my seat belt and harness fully intact.

As fear began to grip me, Psalm 46:10 KJV, "Be still, and know that I am God," thundered into my mind. As I whispered it, an all-encompassing and indescribable peace surrounded me. "Thank You, God. I'm alive!" I breathed.

I awoke to the gentle stroking of my face by a young, good-looking man who was reaching through the window. (God knew what would wake me up!) He was speaking words of intense comfort to me. Never have I been able to recall what he said, but I vividly remember the nurturing and calmness that accompanied it.

"My name is Jeenie Gordon. I've been at a retreat in the mountains at Forest Home Conference Center," I said. "This is Saturday, the sixteenth of August," I continued. "What's your name?"

"Steve," he answered.

"Steve, I'm scared. I'm all alone. Will you stay with me?" I queried. He nodded.

In retrospect, no one would have been allowed in the ravine who was not a uniformed, authorized person. Steve was in street clothes. I am fully convinced that Steve was an angel of the Lord sent to minister to me in my need.

"Here's your identification," the policeman said as he handed my wallet through the shredded glass.

Paramedics and officers converged on my car. "Now, we want you to stay very still. We can't get you out, so we're going to call another team. We'll have to take you out through the roof. They'll be here soon," said one paramedic.

With somber expression, he continued, "I've never seen an accident this bad where anybody lived."

(Later I viewed the pictures of my annihilated car. The driver's side was destroyed and the roof smashed into the steering column. I realized the only spot where I could have survived was the passenger's side. It was my place of safety, where God gently moved me, seat belt and all.)

The additional paramedics arrived and were on top of my car. "Okay, where does it hurt?" they asked.

"Nowhere," I said. After thinking a moment, I responded, "My side. Where the seat belt is hooked." As I unhooked the belt and harness, I watched it retract to the other side.

"All right. Now we're going to put this board behind your back. Don't move, we'll do it," they said.

They formulated their plan and continued instruction. "We've decided to lift you through the roof. You're small, so we'll just reach down and raise you up. Don't move, just relax. We'll do it. We're going to count to three and begin to hoist. Let's go. One, two, three. . . ." At that point, I again went into unconscious-ness and was taken through the roof, up the hill, and placed in the ambulance.

Waking up in the ambulance, I felt chatty. "Hi," I volun-teered.

"Man, that was something. Boy, are you lucky. It's a good thing you were alone and no one else was hurt," the attendant said.

With a twinkle in my eye, I returned, "Oh, I wasn't alone."

Startled, he said, "You weren't?"

"Nope. God was with me," I declared.

Smiling, he quipped, "Yes, He sure was. He sure was."

At the emergency room, doctors and nurses were buzzing around me. "She's a living miracle. It's amazing, just amazing, she's alive and awake." The story spread rapidly.

As I was being wheeled to the X-ray room, I began scratching my head. Dirt was falling out in clumps. "Yuck, my hair is so dirty," I remarked to the nurse as I continued scraping.

"Honey, you're alive and a miracle—your hair will wash," she wisely answered.

By the time I got to the X-ray room and moved around from table to table, I was beginning to be stiff and felt as if I'd been hit by a truck. The technician was a huge, gentle man. I stood about halfway up his arm. Finally, he picked me up and moved me from place to place. What a relief.

Then I waited for the reading of the X rays. Soon the attending doctor came in. He gently held my hand and said, "The X rays show you have extensive kidney damage, and we will need to operate tonight to remove your kidney." With a pat on my arm, he left the room.

An incredible fear gripped me. I was alone and terrified. Grabbing the side of the table, I said, "God, I'm alive and even if they remove my kidney, I'm going to trust You." I felt the overwhelming peace of His love surrounding me—a calmness that was beyond my comprehension.

When a nurse entered, I said, "Would you please call my daughter? Tell her I'm okay. I want her to come, but not alone. Tell her to bring a friend."

When she arrived, I saw the fright on her face and said, "Kathi, I'm all right."

Afterward she said, "Mom, your face looked so gray. I was really scared."

Further examination of the X rays suggested that perhaps my kidney was only bruised, so the doctor decided to wait until morning to perform surgery.

It turned out my kidney was bruised and no surgery was necessary. During my hospital stay of six days, I experienced love from family, friends, and staff in huge doses. There have been no physical problems resulting from the accident. God totally protected me.

## A Future and a Hope

At this writing, my eyes brim with tears and my heart is full of thanks to my miracle-working God.

A passage of Scripture that has permeated my life is Jeremiah 29:11 NAS: " 'For I know the plans that I have for you,' declares the Lord, 'plans for welfare and not for calamity to give you a future and a hope.' "

We have a God we can trust, if we are willing to release ourselves to Him totally.

Following the dark days of my separation/divorce, as I began to experience healing and learn the value of trust, I penned these lines:

I'll Exchange

Illusive happiness for indescribable peace,
Empty success for the lessons in defeat,
Overpowering sunlight for refreshing rain,
Majestic mountains for valleys,
Comfort for the growth in pain
                        because
        I'm willing to trust You—
in my defeat
                during the rain of life, and
                        through my dark valleys!

# Insight for Growth

I challenge you to pray this prayer with me:

Dear Father,
   At this moment I give my life to You—totally. Take me.
Forgive me. Make me whole.
   Turn this tragedy around. Help me to trust You to bring
good into my life.
   I am Yours forever.
   Amen.

Jeenie Gordon is available for speaking engage-
ments. She may be contacted at the following
address:

New Hope Counseling
908 South Village Oak Drive
Suite 250
Covina, CA 91724
(818) 967-6421